INTRODUCTION

C000262887

Every year since 2005 kayakers have been lured north for a special weekend that gives them   ⌐cuand's premier playboat river, the Inverness-shire Garry, on the Saturday and the beautiful but intir   ...g ivlorriston on the Sunday. The event, rapidly becoming a canoeing institution, is now dubbed 'The Wet West Paddle Fest'.

Probably most come simply to get the chance to run these rivers. Both are dam controlled and when they release offer quality paddling in the semi-arid conditions that afflict Highland Scotland each summer. The Morriston releases for twenty-four hours from mid-day Tuesday each week, which isn't at all convenient for a weekend jaunt. The Garry has consistently presented far greater difficulties and has been the scene of one of Scotland's most protracted conflicts between kayakers and anglers.

Once among Scotland's finest salmon rivers, fished by the rich and famous, the Garry was dammed for hydro-electricity in the 1950s. The redds, or gravel beds where the salmon laid their eggs in the head waters of the river, were destroyed, reducing the fishing to a shadow of its former glory. Nevertheless, water has to be released once a week in summer to keep the river alive. These 'freshets' still attract the occasional angler and although the river has long been paddled the main growth in its popularity stemmed from the short boat revolution of the 1990s. For many years there was a predictable twenty-four hour release which drew boaters in increasing numbers on a summer's evening from as far afield as the grim concrete canyons of central Scotland. It became increasingly clear there was little evidence that there were any fish to catch, a source of much angst to the river owner, Paul Williamson, who was busily trying to sell permits to catch very little. Stories are told of angry Belgian anglers waving shotguns at hordes of youths in colourful plastic boats. Down on the river things weren't much better. The eddy beside the playwave would be full to overflowing with midge food patiently waiting a turn. Anyone who screwed up and didn't get a good ride would be very badly chewed before the next opportunity arose. One absurdly tall boater seemed to rise above all this. Surveying the scene he would announce, with amused disdain, that "It's a zoo" and then ride the wave for a seeming eternity while desperados in the eddy fought for space to roll and wash off the insect life.

Andy Jackson had been coming to the river ever since he was a gangly teenager, blythly ignoring all demands that he should go away. He became the river adviser, engaging in long and ultimately futile negotiations over access. Mr Williamson wanted to impose limits on the numbers who could paddle the river at any one time, to exclude paddlers until 6 pm when the midges' feeding frenzy peaks and from below Whitebridge. Jackson was personally unwilling to accept any of these restrictions and eventually Mr Williamson refused to continue negotiating with him and persuaded the electricity company to instigate a programme of random releases. Numbers of kayakers fell dramatically. Few were willing to drive all the way from Glasgow to find a dry gulch. A system of espionage and intelligence gathering of such deviousness, cunning and marginal legality that its details cannot be revealed enabled local boaters to enjoy all but exclusive use of Scotland's best play river. These were the famine years for those most affectionate of insects, the Glen Garry midges.

On the face of things, this should have suited Jackson. He could have the river to himself but he continued to advocate open access, both privately and publicly. By the time of his untimely death he had played a significant part in the creation of the Scottish Access Code which, among other things, recognised the right of paddlers to responsible access to rivers. The random releases continue on the Garry but most people are able to suss out when there will be water. The access code effectively ended the campaign to limit the numbers paddling at any one time or to keep them above Whitebridge.

There were about 500 people at the memorial service after his funeral, some from as far away as Canada and New Zealand. There was a familiar smile on the grainy image on the sheet that simply said 'Andy Jackson 25th May 1971 – 5th December 2004'.

"Andy Jackson was a terrible man..." said the minister, pausing for effect.
"He was terribly kind." Another pause.
"He was terribly tall."
"He was terribly principled."
"He was terribly brave." ... "He was terribly sharp." ... "He was terribly caring." ... "He was terribly vibrant."

In front of the her in the packed church after the interment was a gathering of people clearly struggling to come to terms with their loss. Seriously hard people, mountain guides, cutting edge paddlers, paragliders and crazy skiers were visibly red eyed and emotional. The minister could see this.

"It would be insensitive of me and downright untrue to suggest that you will all get over the death of Andy. You will not. You will learn to live with it and in time you will see that he has a part still to play in the present."

The first Garry and Morriston weekend ran in March 2005. Paul Williamson generously forgot his differences with Andy and agreed to a Saturday dam release and has done so in the two subsequent years. No more fitting memorial could be created to a man who relished parties and the company of others on rivers. The event continues and in time it may be forgotten how it ever got started. Andy Jackson, however, played a major part in the development of Scottish whitewater boating. His legacy goes far beyond an annual event of adrenaline laden paddling and is a story well worth recounting.

CONTENTS

ANDY AND BRIDGET SURFING ON THE WORLD TOUR. BELOW, IN FETCHING MATCHING GEAR.

BOY MEETS GIRL

Bridget Thomas is an Essex girl whose parents inexplicably neglected to call Sharon.

She began paddling at the age of ten. Educated in a girls' only grammar school, there was little else to absorb her attention. By the time she went up to Cambridge she was already a Division One slalom paddler and had been competing all over Europe since the tender age of 16. At Cambridge she progressed to Women's Premier Division, won the British Universities Slalom and Whitewater Race and was annually awarded a triple blue for her troubles. She also found time to play rugby but cannot remember whether she won a half blue or not.

Clearly a formidable talent, she harboured secret anxieties about big whitewater, bigger, that is, than one might encounter on a Premier Division slalom course. This was all about to change. In the summer of '92 Bridget set off with her boyfriend on an Alpine kayaking holiday only to blunder into seriously bad company in a riverside campsite. Roddy Webster and Chris Dickinson were there with half the contents of a student flat from Dundee, namely Neil the Psycho, Fozzie and AJ, one Andy Jackson on his first alpine kayaking trip, although he had already been to Nepal. Some of the people in the flat used their real names but, in the case of others, their student radical activities might well explain a reluctance to do so, even on the continent, where they were ulikely to encounter members of the Tayside Constabulary. Like Lenin, Trotsky and other Bolsheviks in pre-revolutionary Russia they may have felt their survival depended on pseudonyms.

The trip involved the inevitable full-on boating. Dickinson recalls running the Swiss gorges on the Inn. "Four sections in one day and Andy and Rod did it all in the Duo including a drop we portaged and we also ripped up the Oetz, three sections in a day and the Trisanna, Sanna, Inn, etc. We ran the Fliess section on a sudden dam release that caught us out on the Inn and Bid had a giant swim in her diminutive slalom buoyancy aid! She seemed to need to follow someone all the time to get a line."

Of these assorted hooligans Bridget felt the greatest affinity to Roddy Webster, older, perhaps more mature, more sensible than the rest. She goes so far as to describe him as good looking, witty and charming. Jackson was perhaps too outré for an otherwise respectable young lady from Cambridge University. Whatever happened on that trip, and significant whitewater was certainly part of it, she seemed to have wanted more. Nice girls, it is said, are often attracted to a bit of old rough. On her return to England Miss Thomas organised herself a place on an environmental project for the long term unemployed, an unlikely learning opportunity for one with a good honours degree in Natural Sciences from Clare. The project was based in Dundee and featured useful skills such as fencing, ditching, tree planting and putting up nest boxes. Roddy Webster found an earlier offer to put her up inconvenient but told her that Andy Jackson would happily house her. Nobody told Jackson about this but that wasn't really a problem as Andy was driven by an urge to accommodate the world's homeless, usually in houses belonging to other people. Nobody with a kayak was ever knowingly turned away. He was, it seems, more than a little pleased to renew his acquaintance with Bid. To put it simply, he had fancied her from the start but, remarkably, had been too shy to say so. Some flat inmates found it difficult to adjust to this new reality. They had been living happily together, a band of brothers united against the innumerable iniquities of the world, when suddenly this posh bird alighted and took possession of the alpha male. It quite took their breath away.

Andy's Scottish Nationalism was never racist, his own father is English, and Bridget's ethnicity was never a problem. She was simply annexed as an asset of the putative Scottish state and was thereafter referred to as a Scottish paddler; partial reparation for the theft of the Stone of Destiny and Berwick-on-Tweed. Paul Currant and Andy England later received similar treatment.

In the weeks and months that followed Andy and Bridget paddled three or more times a week on all the good rivers that can be accessed from Dundee, the Essex girl growing more and more confident on big water and steep wee burns. In the summer of '93 they were persuaded to go to the Nottingham Holme Pierrepont Rodeo by Glasgow University medical student, Paul Currant. Paul had already been selected for the British men's rodeo team in the forthcoming world championships in the States and when Bridget won the women's competition she was offered a wild card entry, the women's team having already been selected. Had Andy entered the rodeo scene earlier he would have been in the team but selection had already taken place and there was much more competition for men's places. At Notts they met Shaun Baker and Team Worzell for the first time. More rodeo followed. Bridget remembers the Bitches rodeo from this era but, improbably, cannot remember whether she won or not. Shaun's memory of Andy at this stage is of a relaxed confident individual. While other competitors sat tense and stony faced in the eddy, awaiting their turn, drinking Red Bull and eating bananas, Jackson chatted and cracked jokes, happily told people what moves he was going to try, and then did them. It would be wrong to say that he wasn't competitive. It was just that the needs to socialise and have fun were as important to him to as the results. Bridget later remarked that for Andy there was no point in just winning if he wasn't having fun. To drive most of the length of Britain and back and not interact with other people would have been an odd thing for Andy to do. He wasn't the man to take himself, or life, too seriously.

The video of the '93 world champs on the Occoee river, Tennessee makes fascinating viewing. The production team were sure that the women's title was between a German, Hannah Swayze, and an American girl, Roxanne McDonough who won all the attention of the camera crew. Finally they had to announce that the women's world championship had been won by Bridget Thomas from a little known country off the coast of France to whom all of 15 seconds of video had been devoted. The bookies dream came true, a total outsider had won the Grand National. Paul Currant was the highest placed of the British men but wasn't happy with his position.

Playboating and rodeo have come a long way since 1993 when Bridget was paddling a 3m+ Prijon Hurricane. The Americans took the rest of the world by surprise with cartwheels, a move that the Brits had never seen before. Fortunately for Bridget the American girl hadn't achieved complete mastery of this new and radical move. As well as sessions doing cool moves in a hole there was a slalom style section which was meat and drink to a Premier Division Paddler and which the Bid was able to win convincingly. This put considerable pressure on the opposition and may account for at times unambitious performances in the hole-playing sessions where some well executed spins, surfing and enders would suffice to secure a high position. In the semi-final Bid blew a kiss to the judges as she dropped into the hole. *Paddler* described her as exuberant, laughing, smiling, and bringing an air of joviality to her rides. In contrast Roxanne looked serious, determined and in control throughout the competition. Although the American won the playboating final by two points Bridget's lead in the slalom gave her the title. Shaun Baker offered his congratulations and said she would never need to buy gear again, which has proved to be almost true. Slalom had given Bid a tough focused, competitive mentality. Paddling with Andy had given her the confidence she needed to play on the big water. She happily acknowledges it as a major factor in her success. For months to come she would be referred to, with appropriate deference, as "the World Champion". Bridget's acquisition represented a significant national triumph. As Andy wasn't too tied up in the competition it gave him the chance to sneak away and paddle an Eastern US river called The Green, a river with a reputation.

It is often said that playboating and rodeo were not Jackson's forte. This is difficult to believe for anybody who has watched him in, say, the Garry playhole, throwing a dozen or more consecutive cartwheels, discarding his paddles and hand surfing, hand rolling and spinning. After a while the audience would start to wonder when he would get bored and give somebody else a turn. He came seventeenth in the 1994 pre-Worlds, a competition which his close friend, Paul Currant, won. Coming seventeenth in the world in a discipline that wasn't his main strength goes some way towards indicating the stature of the man.

So who was this tall gangly lad who had played a major part in Bridget's success? Graeme Jackson, his father, should know better than most.

Andy's childhood –
a father remembers

For one who was so determinedly Scottish, Andrew (he was always Andrew to us, the name Andy came later), was born with two significant birth defects that he had trouble coming to terms with. The first was that he was born in Wales. And if that wasn't bad enough, he had an English father. However, the full awfulness of this situation did not become a burden until his late teens!

He arrived on 25th May 1971 in the Maelor General Hospital at Wrexham in North Wales. The family, my wife Kate and daughter Claire, then aged 16 months, and I were living in Rhydymwyn, just outside Mold, where I was working as a very junior, and recently qualified, Land Agent. In those days Dads were not encouraged, or even allowed, to attend the birth of their children, so I left Kate to get on with it and went to work in the usual way. Looking back it seems incredible, but I wandered into the ward after work to see if there was any progress, and even then had to wait for some hours before being summoned to meet my new son. We moved back to Scotland in 1972.

Babyhood was uneventful for Andrew, apart from his being very slow to potty train!

He had a dramatic visit to his grandparents in Edinburgh for his second Christmas. I would not have believed it had I not seen it, but he managed to put his head through the banisters, which were of cast iron, and anything but flexible. Short of calling the Fire Brigade he could only be extracted by being turned upside down and around. His head was again facing the landing, allowing his ears to slide through the narrow space. Even this maneouvre was significantly delayed by his Uncle Hugh, who insisted on fetching his camera to record the event. We have the photo to this day.

In 1975, after a short time in a large period house in the village of Houston near Paisley, we were able to buy a redundant farm steading about a mile out of the village. Andrew was in his natural element. There was scope here for even his active imagination – trees to climb, a stream to paddle in, fields to explore, a large garden for football (not that Andrew was ever really very interested in anything involving a ball), and empty farm buildings where he could, and did, construct whatever was his fancy at the time.

Our family life has never been exactly straightforward, and our move to Cleaves Farm was no exception. To start with the house was uninhabitable. Our solution was to bring onto the site a 36ft residential caravan and to live in it for the best part of two years. We also managed to time the arrival of a third baby, our daughter Wendy, to coincide with the very day that we moved into the caravan. But wee Andrew, then aged four, took this all in his stride. Perhaps the experience scarred him emotionally, but if so he never let on.

We had a happy team of builders who did most of the conversion work. This was just as well considering the size of the job they had to do. But they were never short of a small boy to give advice and distract them while working. Andrew was fascinated by the activity around him, the cement mixer rumbling away all day and the frequent arrival of lorries carrying all sorts of interesting things. When it was the weekend and the 'men' did not come to entertain him, there was always his dad who needed his help to knock down the old tin sheds and cart them away. He took his 'work' very seriously indeed, and heaven help anyone who had the temerity to suggest that I could do it without him.

Eventually it was finished, or at least the budget was all spent, which was not quite the same thing. The caravan went and he had his own room in the new house. This was just as well, as we had decided to continue the enlargement of our family, slightly unconventionally, by first fostering and then adopting two little boys and a baby girl. Marita, the baby, arrived aged ten months, when Andrew was six. Kevin arrived, aged six, when Andrew was seven and Arthur arrived, aged four, when Andrew was ten. We never had any concerns that Andrew would be put out or hurt by the arrival of these newcomers. He had from an early age shown that unflappability that was to be such a feature of his personality. He just smiled, and went out of his way to include all of them, and it cannot always have been easy, in his various projects. He was always the peacemaker, but very good at winding up his big sister Claire.

Andrew was a very self contained little boy. He would play for hours by himself, quite happily engaged in whatever he was doing at the time. As he grew older his projects became more ambitious, and if assistance were needed he would ask first his siblings, failing which his friend from school, Ian Morgan, and as a last resort, his parents. In his teenage years this independence could be hard for us to accept, but it got easier as we came to trust that, whatever the outcome, Andrew had everything in hand.

At the age of sixteen he fixed his own work experience, at Ardentinny Outdoor Centre, and never looked back. They gave him the opportunity to learn to drive, at the government's expense, and his new driving license gave him the freedom of Scotland in a series of very dilapidated vehicles. (Note that his father had already paid for a course of driving lessons, but the near death of two old ladies, who had the misfortune to be on the pavement at the spot where Andrew was demonstrating his three point turn to the examiner, put paid to any chance of a Pass on that occasion.)

It was Ian Morgan who Andrew roped in to create what he hoped would be the fastest buggy in the world. They scrounged wheels from old prams, timber and various nuts and bolts, and the vehicle took shape in the old byre. Sadly it entirely failed to live up to its creators' expectations, managing only a very modest speed down the farm road. Undaunted, the pair decided to dress it up as a 'moon buggy,' and enter the Fancy Dress Parade at the Kirk Carnival. They even persuaded brother Kevin to join the team, as pilot, because neither of them was small enough to squeeze into the cockpit. So, dressed in green clothes, with green paint to all exposed skin, they pushed it to the village, and entered as 'Martians'. Sad to relate, the organisers were unconvinced that this magnificent entry was the work of the children, so it was judged as ineligible for any of the prizes. Andrew proved, once again, that he was a very uncompetitive person. He showed no disappointment, much to our admiration, even though his parents were gutted.

Early in our life at Cleaves Farm Andrew insisted that we construct a substantial tree house in a large sycamore that stood in the corner of the garden. It had to be at least three metres from the ground, and accommodate at least three people. I may have been the builder but the architect was Andrew. He had some difficulty in accepting that the structure had the limitations of being constructed from half a dozen old doors, and a sheet of corrugated iron, so turrets, trapdoors, and a portcullis were not really an option! Still, once it was built he was most impressed. I am sure the hours he spent in it demonstrated that his ever lively imagination had worked its magic, transforming the hut into whatever was required at the time.

Later, when Andrew was perhaps eleven or twelve, he and a friend constructed a considerably more elaborate 'den' in the corner of the paddock. It was created, with much labour and even more fun, by excavating the hole left by a fallen tree and raising walls around the perimeter. It was roofed and floored with old tin, planks of wood, and any old doors that could be found. In one corner there was a hole in the wall that overlooked the field, and in another was a fireplace. Typically, the boys made absolutely no provision for a chimney, so, when the fire was ceremoniously lit it was not long before the occupants emerged, coughing and spluttering, to get away from the smoke. Shortly after the wooden floor was well alight, to be followed, in short order, by the total destruction of the whole structure. Still, it did make a lovely bonfire.

Andrew started school at the local primary when he was five. Each morning he and his big sister went down to the end of the farm road, a distance of perhaps a quarter of a mile, to be picked up by the school taxi. The system worked well, except the driver, trying to be fair to his passengers, always dropped off first those who he picked up first. This meant the Jacksons, last to be picked up in the morning, were always last to be dropped off after school and this took a good half hour of valuable play time!

Andrew took to school like a duck to water, although he was never a scholar. His tables were a real problem for him, but he tackled them with dogged determination, and the incentive of an Action Man Tower when he could recite them perfectly. For Andrew, anything with Action Man connotations was like honey to a bear. He had a collection of them, fully equipped with all the essential accessories, ropes, guns, vehicles, boats, costumes, radios – in fact the lot. Action Man even took part in the Village Carnival, and was featured as 'Jack climbing the Beanstalk' on the Best Decorated Car Competition of 1979. He won!

Action Man also had to have space in Andrew's bedroom. But as the room was on the small side, and as space also had to be allocated for a fairly complicated train set, the obvious solution was to raise the bed about 1.6 metres from the floor by constructing a platform on which a mattress was placed. This arrangement may have allowed him to utilise all the available floor space, but it made it impossible to make the bed without climbing up onto it! Details like this never seemed to bother Andrew, but drove his mother to distraction!

One day Kate and I were told, by a breathless six year old Andrew, that his sister, Claire, was 'drowning' in the burn. Claire would have been seven. He panted out his message, pointing across the field in the direction of the burn. I have never run so fast in my life. What did I find? Claire, in water that did not come over the top of her Wellington boots, stuck in the mud and waiting patiently for her parents to come to rescue her. She had sent her wee brother back for help, and the story had evidently grown in the time that it took him to reach the house!

Perhaps that occasion was in Kate's mind when he arrived, panting, back at the house at a time when she was about to put the lunch on the table. It must have been a Saturday because Andrew and I had been to Greenock for the morning, where we had manned the telephone in my office – something I did on a rota basis. On the way home we had had a minor crunch in the car; a white van had come out of a turning without looking. My car could not be driven, so a passing friend, who had limited room in his car, had offered to take Andrew back to get Kate to come and fetch me. Did Kate believe her son when he told her about "Dad's crash"? It was some little time later that the true situation was appreciated!

One of the advantages of life in the country was that it was easy for the children to have pets. We had the usual, dogs, cats, pony, hamsters, gerbils, ducks and hens. Andrew insisted on 'adopting' a duck. He gave it a name, and I think he believed that it knew his voice. It certainly did not run away from him as fast as the others did. The ducks were destined for the dinner table, but there the wheels came off the plan. Catching a duck and killing it, before plucking it and dressing it, is the kind of task that falls to father, and this case was no different. My only instructions from Kate were that I was not to kill Andrew's duck, nor let any of the children watch. The last was easy, but in my anxiety I got the birds mixed up and the carcass, proudly produced to the cook, was condemned as 'Oh no. Not THAT one!' Andrew's duck was no more! He was distraught.

One day we had been conscious that it was awfully quiet upstairs, where Andrew was reputedly in his room. All was explained when Action Man descended past the kitchen window, being slowly lowered on a long piece of string from the bedroom above. And he descended not vertically, but laterally, on what Andrew described as his 'Death Slide'. I am sure that Action Man found it much more relaxing than being fired, by catapult, into the air, to demonstrate the effectiveness of his parachute. Sadly the parachute had a poor strike rate when it came to operational efficiency, and Action Man frequently came down much faster than he went up!

It was probably this example that prompted Andrew to demand that I make him his own 'Death Slide'. So we selected a large tree at one side of the paddock to be the take off point, and another, rather smaller tree, on the other side of the paddock, to be the anchor point. Then we went to the docks together and scrounged a 50m length of heavy wire rope, and a pulley to run on it. A tower of scaffolding at the take off to give the necessary height, a seat to ride on, and a rope sling to arrest the seat before it could actually collide with the anchor tree, completed the job. The resulting slide was an enormous success. What the Health and Safety Inspectorate would have made of it I dread to think.

Andrew was not always so courageous, however. I remember the way that he would insist on watching the early episodes of 'Dr Who and the Daleks', but only from behind the sofa! And he was not at all brave when watching the televised movie 'Jaws' at the age of seven or eight, which gave him nightmares for some time after. Likewise he did not enjoy his early Boys Brigade camps because one of the officers told the boys ghost stories late into the evening – stupid man!

Where he always scored, however, was in the self confidence stakes. He was never reluctant to take on new challenges, or to go into unfamiliar situations. As a teenager he would be the one who was prepared to go into a strange café and find some new friends, or to venture into places that his siblings were reluctant to explore. Even on holiday in France, (and his language skills were abysmal), he would act as escort for his big sister until she felt comfortable with the people they had met, at which point Andrew would be dispensed with and sent back the caravan.

When Andrew was coming up to his tenth birthday we thought it was about time that he was introduced to the Scottish hills, and for his birthday party we marched him, about five friends, and his brother Kevin, up Ben Lomond. It was a great success, even if it did rain much of the way down and from then on Andrew was as keen on his hillwalking as his mother. I would like to say that the whole family got the bug, but that would be a gross exaggeration as only Kate has ever completed the Munros. Indeed the rest of us have little interest in this activity.

Each summer holidays, from when Andrew was eight until he was fifteen, we would take the entire family to Gairloch for two and sometimes three weeks' camping. The campsite at Big Sands stands behind the dunes and is large enough

to absorb even the Jackson Family. It had and probably still has clean toilets, a small shop and very little else. But the beach and the area generally drew us back year after year. Andrew was never at a loss for something to do, whatever the weather. He and his sister Claire always had a gaggle of younger children who they would organise for games, competitions, barbeques, explorations, and cycle rides. As the children grew older we would take canoes, wind surfers, and one year even a small sailing dinghy.

In 1987 we were about to set off for Gairloch as usual, when Andrew announced that a friend had 'sat on' his arm, and that it was a 'bit sore'. Off to casualty for the fracture to be set and plastered! So Andrew's water sports were severely restricted that year. (He did try wearing a large rubber glove, but it didn't solve the problem.) Fortuitously we met, quite by chance, a family from England who had a holiday house at Badachro, not far away. The 'Cripps' were delightful and were keen hill walkers. They let Andrew join their assaults on all of the major peaks in the area, including the Fisherfields. This experience of the wilderness areas seemed to set the seal on Andrew's love of the outdoors. Telling of it later he recalled that he had the best holiday ever.

We did manage to find a sport that all of us could do, and enjoy, and that was canoeing. We bought a fibreglass kayak at, of all places, the Royal Highland Show, and carried it home on the roof of the car. A visit to Castle Semple Loch quickly persuaded us that this was what we had been looking for and I was sent back to Ingliston to buy two more of the same. One of these survives to this day in the back garden, and is still used occasionally. Needless to say, once he had joined the Lochwinnoch Kayak Club, and achieved his two star award, these boats were not good enough for our Andrew, so a more 'professional' boat was needed. We still have that one too, but Andrew quickly progressed to boats of half the size and four times the price!

We used to go, as a family, to Johnstone High School, where the club had the facility to use the swimming pool for an evening each week. There we were drilled in the finer points of canoeing, how to capsize without actually drowning, etc. I think we all got our one star award, but only Andrew and Wendy went on to the two star, let alone the three star. At which point Andrew started as a trainee at Ardentinny Outdoor Centre, where Chris Dickinson took over from where John Webster had left off – and the rest, as they say, is history.

For his secondary education Andrew attended Gryffe High School in Houston. He showed, at twelve, no sign of the growth that was such a feature of his late teens, indeed he was on the small side for his age. He was such a mild mannered boy that he had to put up with some bullying at school. Although we all acknowledged this as happening, Andrew never allowed any adult intervention. It seemed to diminish after the first year. Looking back on it, we suspect that the catalyst for this friction was the mixing, for the first time, of children from the two villages of Houston and Bridge of Weir. Whatever the reason, Gryffe High School coped, as did our Andrew.

When Andrew was in his early teens he had a tendency to bump into things – graceful was never a term that could describe him! When he went into a roomful of seated people it was common for us to notice that everyone there would unconsciously draw in their feet, and tuck them under their chairs, lest they be tripped over or trodden on. His gangly frame would stand out in any physical activity, which probably explains his strong dislike of any kind of team sport, unless it involved water. So it was strange to see him take such pleasure, and to become so expert, in skiing.

All through his teenage years Andrew went skiing at Glenshee with Ski Coaching Renfrew at every possible opportunity, which was not all that often as there were financial constraints. It was on one such trip that he achieved fame, or notoriety, by colliding with the queue of skiers waiting to join the tow, and demolishing it! His excessive enthusiasm, speed, and a noticeable lack of control, led to at least one casualty being sent on their way to hospital. Andrew never quite forgave himself for that incident, especially as it was witnessed by his big sister. But it didn't deter him from skiing, and as his skills increased he became an expert, if not stylish, skier. It suited his love of the great outdoors and provided an outlet for his abundant energy during the winter months when canoeing or sailing were not an option.

One New Year, I think it would have been in 1986, he persuaded the whole family to go to Aviemore for Hogmanay. Although our caravan was not small, and we did sometimes squash all eight of us into it, plus dog, Andrew elected to demonstrate his hardy independence by opting to sleep in the caravan awning rather than the van itself. It was nearly dawn when the door opened and this frozen boy staggered into the caravan in a fairly advanced state of hypothermia! We simply had not realised just how cold it was. Fortunately there was no lasting damage, or perhaps this incident accounts for a lot!

BREAKING OUT

"I actually taught Andy to canoe when he was but a mere midge of a kid, he really was once short."

(GARY FAWCETT, LOCHWINNOCH AND PAISLEY KAYAK CLUB)

1986 CASTLE SEMPLE. ANDY THE FLEDGELING KAYAKER.

By 1987 the fledgling was ready to fly the nest. Keen to pursue a career in outdoor education he secured a training placement at Strathclyde Council's Ardentinny Centre where Chris Dickinson remembers him arriving as a good, solid two star paddler. The Centre principal, Nick Halls, organised funding for Andy and another lad of his age, Alan Burt, from a government initiative, the Youth Training Scheme (YTS). To many YTS was considered a scheme designed to keep unemployment figures down so as not to embarrass the Thatcher Government. Many of the placements looked pointless. One young woman from Tain was taught to operate a mini-digger. This might appear to be good, equal opportunities stuff but what she really wanted, above all else, was to be a hairdresser. She hated mud. Other placements seemed designed only to provide employers with cheap young labour. Andy and Alan would do better than many. Dickinson remembers that they both joined Cowal Kayak Club and were keen to learn and help. "We were just starting competitive polo when they arrived. They threw themselves into that. We played there every week. Alan was better than Andy at this point. Andy made second team, Alan the first. Andy's sister Wendy sometimes came and played with us too. Andy was tall, wide-eyed and very proper. He was well mannered, did not swear, was very naïve and very enthusiastic. He and Alan were keen to learn any new skills but especially kayaking. I recall at that time coaching Andy on four star skills at Eachaig River; we often made evening visits to the weir there or on the river if high. He was promising."

In his own way Andy remained very proper. He might take on some of the personality traits of some of the more uncouth people he operated with but at heart he remained the polite middle class boy from one of Glasgow's more desirable suburbs. Bridget played a bit of rugby at Cambridge and learned most of the songs associated with that game. To her surprise she discovered that Andy didn't like her singing them one little bit. It would be hard to imagine Andy's mother, Kate, a respectable solicitor, singing such songs, so clearly family values continued to influence him. By way of contrast, Andy and Bridget used to read to each other from time to time. Listening to Bridget reading from Irvine Welsh's 'Train Spotting', he relished what he described as her "posh Cambridge voice," rendering the coarsest outbursts of deprived and depraved central Scotland.

When Jackson went to Ardentinny whitewater boating was at a critical stage in its evolution, moving from four metre long glass fibre or early Tupperware craft to much shorter rotomoulded plastic boats. Developments in mountaineering and climbing are very well documented because of the sports custom of recording first ascents. Kayaking lacks this and has never developed the literary tradition of climbing. This makes it almost impossible to quantify the achievements of an exploratory paddler or to assess where the sport had reached at any given time. The big volume rivers such as the Tay, Tweed, Clyde and Spey were familiar to canoeists in the years before the Second World War and could be paddled in fabric or plywood craft. When glass fibre boats became common in the sixties the range of river that could be navigated increased exponentially. This would be the era when the more stimulating sections of the Orchy, the Findhorn and Spean Gorges started to be frequently paddled. Glass Reinforced Plastic (GRP) boats are in fact extremely tough and ideally suited to big flow rivers. If built heavy they can take quite big hits and have the virtue of being relatively easy to repair. German paddlers began to experiment with short high volume boats that could survive steeper Alpine torrents but these rarely made an appearance on Scottish rivers. Everests, based on the boats used by the Mike Jones 1976 descent of the Duhd Kosi, did become fairly common and edged the sport in the direction of steeper and rockier drainage features. Plastic boats began to make an impact from the early 1980s, opening up rivers that would have previously destroyed boats. It was probably about this time that the Etive was first paddled and perhaps, too, the Falls of Dochart and the Leny. The Lochhead and Todd guide of 1986 describes the Etive fairly fully and with great respect, mentions the possibility of paddling dangerous falls in the Roy Gorge and implies that the Upper Nevis, above Poll Dubh, is to be avoided. Sadly the history of river exploration at this time is scarcely documented. English paddlers made frequent forays north and ran what they found. Chris Dickinson spent much time sussing out the Allt a' Chaorainn, one of the Etive's famous tributaries. After launching unmanned craft as probes down the more intimidating section he finally paddled believing that nobody else had been there before. Later, in conversation with Mike Hayward, he discovered that the Lakeland paddler had done it in the early 1980s. In the late 1980s another group of southern boaters set out to paddle all the rivers of Sutherland, a trip which ended with the sad death of one of the group on an unscouted descent of Fatal Fall on the Oykell. At the time they believed that they had made the first descent of the Falls of Shin which local boaters, paddling Dancers and protected by skateboard helmets, had been running as a short adrenalin fix for some time. Chris Dickinson thinks he may have been first to paddle the Kiachnish, the Coe, and the Upper Nevis with Iain Hamilton, and the Leven with John Hough and Graeme Togwell but there is no way he can be sure of this. Exploratory paddlers tended to operate as isolated little groups, preferring to keep their burns secret and resenting any publicising of good rivers. Dundee's Roddy Webster was probably the arch exponent of the secrecy approach. Sam Crymble, first from the Loch Eil Centre near Fort William and then from Glenmore Lodge near Aviemore, took advantage of being geographically well positioned to run new rivers. It was into this murky and secretive world that Dickinson would initiate Jackson. The potential for new boating and first descents was ripe and ready for exploitation. There was truth in the saying "Cometh the hour, cometh the man". For steep creek boating in the Highlands that man would be Andy Jackson.

THE MENTOR,
THE MOUNTAIN BAT & BEYOND...

Chris introduced Andy to the state of the art Mountain Bat, to steeper rockier rivers, to scanning OS maps for possible new runs, marking of critical contours, calculating gradients, reading whitewater, precision paddling and making every stroke count. Andy would use this reconnaissance system throughout his exploratory paddling career and it served him well.

Chris Dickinson recalls

I worked with Andy as Assistant Instructor from time to time. One week on a mountaineering course he and I were on Ben Lui with a group heading east. As the group followed the trail down Cononish Glen, I wanted to follow the river as I suspected a possible run. Andy came too. Although he was a grade 2 paddler, he was enthused saying "I want to do that." We walked the run at low water and I made notes and diagrams of the difficulties as I usually did. At this time I was beginning to explore a whole range of spate rivers at low water and then make descents later. I worked from OS maps to find sections and hiked them. I'd select gauges and note a good water level and then wait for chance to do the run. Andy got very interested in helping me. We would scout various runs, cut wood out of streambeds and use a winch to pull out old metal objects.

Both Andy and Alan were on centre canoeing courses quite a bit as Nick Halls could see that their skills in that area were increasing rapidly; they got extra time on the water and they were probably sent to Glenmore Lodge on a course or two, and they were sent away for a week of sea paddling with Alan Kimber, all as part of their YTS training.

Back at the Cononish, Andy and Alan came with me a few months later to attempt what we assumed was the first descent. I got hammered in my Topo and swam at the first major drop, getting stuffed in the cave. Alan then did something similar in a Mountain Bat, but he went deep. Andy was on a line with me belaying and he jumped in to get Alan but when he grabbed the boat and turned it over Alan was not in there. Alan came up on far side of pool a funny colour. Andy portaged. We completed the rest of the run, running all the drops. This was probably Andy's first taste of first descent fever.

I trained Andy up on rivers such as the Cur, Kinglas and Orchy most commonly but many other runs besides. Andy was enthusiastic but inconsistent. He would miss critical eddies. However, his rolling was generally good. On a run down the Cur, he ran the main drop backwards. I castigated him, insisting he work harder or "die". We became very good friends and were the most active paddlers in the club. Andy had a whitewater helmet with a homemade faceguard on it that Alan referred to as the "toast rack". He was there on many explorations with folks like Ian Hamilton, Ian Sinclair, Al Lindsay and Graham Togwell. We paddled rivers like the Coe, the Kiachnish, Cononish, Cur, Orchy and its tributaries, the Minnoch, and many many others.

During the summer of 1988, at the end of their year, Andy and Alan came on a paddling trip to Norway with me, Callum Anderson, Mark Turnbull, Pete Surfleet, Gillian Pyle and John Hough. It was a great trip with brilliant levels. Everyone was paddling grade 4–5 river sections and rapids. Andy fell in a pourover, no 'the' pourover, in the Sjoa canyon and with eyes on stalks he cranked his way out. Alan got pummelled on the Jolstra and nearly drowned on the Bua in flood. He was beginning to get out of his depth whilst Andy was beginning to look comfortable. At this time Andy was in a Mountain Bat. I had been the only Topo owner in Scotland for some time and all thought I was crazy and liable to get pummelled as I did from time to time in closed holes at the bottom of steep drops. I took a Mountain Bat to Norway too.

I took Mark and Callum to Nepal as well as Andy, for whom it was his first visit. It was Easter and low water. We ran the upper Bhote Kosi, class 4/5. Then a thunderstorm swelled the Tamba Kosi and we ran this at a much higher than normal level, an epic two day run. We portaged once, a rapid that Andy ran. This was the first time I saw him run something we did not do. We also did the Sun Kosi and the Marsyandi in three days from Syange to Dumre. On that trip Andy waved Callum into a bad hole in which he swam and we gave him stick for waving him in there. As Andy's "coach" I wanted him to develop a skilful but safe style of paddling. He was my main partner in my own aspirations in paddling at this time and I wanted him to be rock solid. Nepal was a mind expander for Andy. On this trip we met Jonas Nocker from Germany, who told me to look up his friend Paul Currant who had recently moved to Glasgow.

Andy, John Hough and I made a river trip to the Appalachians at Easter one year. We flew to Boston with Mountain Bats and were picked up by Andy's Uncle Quentin who loaned us a car. We spent three weeks paddling class 4 and 5 rivers from Pennsylvania to Georgia experiencing a new run every day. For two weeks we paddled with folks from Pennsylvania Kayak Club and their friends and had a ball paddling with folks in a wide range of craft from Dancers, through squirts, composite boats with squirting sterns and open boats. Great trip. Andy almost drove the car off the road in ice and we had to get a new wheel. The whole trip was a pilgrimage to William Nealy land.

Bridget later remarked: "Uncle Quentin complained the car came back with 3,000 extra miles on the clock and stank of wet gear for six months thereafter. On a subsequent trip he did not offer a vehicle to Andy and me".

We were in Spean Bridge paddling one day and driving past the Monessie in flood. Two guys were unloading kayaks above the gorge. We were staggered. We had just been on the dam section. We asked them if they knew where they were. It was Rod Webster and Roddy MacDonald. They said "Spean Gorge" and we corrected them and suggested they came down with us to put in at the foot of the Monessie and do the run below. This they did. We portaged left at the huge grade 5+ and during the portage Rod Mac dropped his boat into a rapid. Webster seal launched into maelstrom and gave chase whilst we got into the river more circumspectly and followed. We all had tea at my chalet and exchanged numbers. This was first time we had either of us met Roddy Webster.

Around this time I called Paul Currant and we met him in Glen Etive one day and ran the Allt a' Chaorainn. We could see right away that Paul was an epic paddler. Andy was totally fascinated by him and at that moment decided he had to get a Topo. Whatever Paul did or had Andy wanted.

ANDY AND SHOVIT 1990

Paul Currant hasn't forgotten his first encounter with the tall boy. "The first time I met him he didn't stop talking from Glasgow to Onich with intermittent singing along to the Corries. I remember meeting him in a lay-by just north of Glasgow in the pissing rain and his 'roof-rack' – a boat shaped dent in the roof of the car." Andy had a succession of 'interesting' cars at this time including a Vauxhall Shovit (Chevette) with a poor starter motor and a road sign covering most of the rusty holes in the floor pan.

LEFT AND ABOVE,
AN EARLY TRIP TO
NORWAY, 1990.

Andy and Chris began to have differences. Andy had come to the conclusion that he needed all his time to go paddling and that he could only do this if he spent very little on food, accommodation or clothes just when Chris was developing a taste for good living. Andy found it also helped if he could get sponsorship for his sport. He was living in Dundee while Chris was on the West Coast. A certain distance crept into what had been a mutually rewarding friendship. Dickinson recalls a trip to Norway, where these differences become apparent. "Andy, Bid, Paul, Rod and a friend of Paul's, Colin, went to Norway with me. We all had Topos, except Rod who had a Rotobat and a C1. Paul also had the new Hurricane. On first day Rod, Paul and Andy were getting stuck into class 5+ gorge runs. I was recovering from shoulder injury so gave that a miss. Those three ran some hard stuff that trip. Colin, Bid and I did some of the rest. A notable descent was the Sjoa Canyon at a 25 year high level. It was surprisingly OK despite the raft companies saying death/grade 6. Towards the end of the trip we stopped a night and rented a cabin as it was wet weather. It was about £5 each. Andy and Bid decided to sleep in a bus shelter. He knew how to treat a lady! I was disturbed on this trip that Andy wanted us not to pay the dirt road tolls whenever possible. I could only see that this would alienate the locals against foreign paddlers."

In his defence Bridget says that Andy's attitude stemmed from his youthful revolutionary, anti-Thatcherite socialism. Back at home he regularly failed to pay to use the Duke of Atholl's estate road up the Tilt on the pretext that it was wrong for one man to own so much of Scotland. On this occasion he seemed to have failed to differentiate between a Norwegian rural community and an absentee Scottish landowner. Later on, when he was no longer an impoverished student, Andy would rethink his attitude on such matters.

If Andy had a sensible Scottish reluctance to part with cash, Bridget would have been scarcely more willing to open her purse. Fifteen years later she remains a traveller with limited need of luxury and a keen sense of budget. She still can't say Loch Lochy but she exhibits other symptoms of the stereo-type Scots character. While she didn't sleep too well that night, she would have been well aware how long they would have to work to earn the £10 they saved by sleeping in the bus shelter. Andy and his mentor were starting to drift apart. Partly it was due to age and partly it was due to diverging values. Although they would paddle together with some regularity for some years a certain tension had crept into the friendship.

Dickinson recalls that he began to see rather less of Andy. "He was becoming much more political and radical. He seemed to want to be involved in militancy. We paddled more occasionally. Around this time I took Andy to the Leven, a river I had been taunting him about for four years, under the name 'Little Corsica'. I wanted to run it before letting him know where it was. I saw Andy as little more than a rival now for first descents. I knew what he had done because he left his 'map' in my car one day. I met him in Glencoe with Mousey Turnbull. I said "today's the day". We blindfolded him and took him to the Leven. We hiked up with only one glimpse of the river and put on. We ran down. I told him to hit the left eddy above the End of the World. Looking at his face as he craned his long neck from the eddy over the edge was one of the highlights of my times with him. All three of us went on to run the End of the World at a pretty high flow; I had previously run it lower."

The apprenticeship was well and truly over. From here on in Andy would be his own man and paddle his own canoe.

ANDY AT THE
TIMEX DISPUTE,
1993.

WILD CHILD

THE STUDENT YEARS

Deep concern has developed in political circles in recent years about the reluctance of the young to engage in politics or even to bother to vote. A brief survey of Andy's political youth might lead the great and the good, the spin doctors and the placemen to the conclusion that apathy has real benefits. Media folk would see it differently. Colourful characters make good news and there are those who say that every functioning democracy needs a gadfly to prick its conscience and remind the masses of the real issues facing humanity.

Andy's parents don't remember him being greatly interested in politics in his school years. By the time he reached Northern College in Dundee this had all changed, probably due to the influence of Nick Halls at the Ardentinny Outdoor Centre. David McGovern, a Scottish National Party activist and who became a close associate of Andy recalls that: "Andy had once kayaked up the Holy Loch to the submarine base in protest at nuclear weapons before he came to Dundee. He was arrested and freed without charge. Even at the start of 1st year, Foz (Richard Salmond) remembers Andy's room in the halls of residence being festooned with political stickers and posters. If not hugely politically active before college then he certainly had a very well developed set of values which then found an environment to develop into political action."

When McGovern first encountered Jackson he told him that he had long wanted to replace the Union Flag on Broughty Castle with something more appropriate. "Right," said Andy, "Let's do it, now". With a ladder borrowed from the college and some climbing gear they invested the outer defences before climbing the walls to get to the flagpole. Soon the famous Dundee Courier carried the news of the invasion.

ACTIVISTS MOUNT 'INVASION' OF BROUGHTY FERRY CASTLE

Banners demanding a vote on Scotland's constitutional future were unfurled at Broughty Castle in the early hours of yesterday after the building was 'invaded' by political activists.

Residents awoke to the sight of a St Andrew's Cross flying on the flagpole usually displaying the Union Jack.

Draped over the castle walls were three banners with the messages, Referendum Now, Let Scotland Choose, and Scotland United Shall Never Be Defeated.

Later a caller to *The Courier* said the banners had been hung about 3am by activists who, he claimed, were not aligned to any party or organisation.

He did, however, say those responsible were supporters of Scotland United. The caller also refused to say how many people were involved in the incident.

By mid-morning only one banner remained on the castle walls, the other two having been removed by police.

A spokesman for Tayside Police explained the Let Scotland Choose banner had been left because officers had been unable to reach it. He said it would be removed from the castle today.

He added that no further action would be taken as no offence had been committed.

The flag was replaced and Jackson arrested paying a second visit to the castle. Tayside Council, who owned the structure, then decided not to restore the Union Flag as it might again become a target for similar pranks. Instead they replaced it with the Saltire which seemed to have popular support locally.

Andy and David helped organise a rally in Dundee's Caird Hall in which Ricky Ross of Deacon Blue and Alex Salmond (SNP) agreed to speak in support of Scotland United, a cross party alliance campaigning for a second referendum. When the very right wing DC Thomson Press refused to advertise the event Jackson and McGovern abseiled down the city chambers building with a banner. Challenged by a police officer at the start Jackson claimed to be cleaning the windows. Grampian TV were on hand to record the event and Thomson Press reported the incident thus advertising the meeting for free, and the crowds rolled in.

One night they painted the slogan 'Let Scotland Choose' on one of the back roads of Angus, which by sheer co-incidence was to be used the next day by John Gummer, Conservative Cabinet Minister, on his way to inspect a military establishment. National Security appeared to have been compromised and penetrated by this lunatic fringe of Scottish politics and appropriate panic ensued. When Andy and David turned up to admire their handiwork in the light of day the place was crawling with armed police looking for bombs. There was also the small matter of the theft of a Union Jack, a symbol deeply offensive to a member of the SNP, from an army recruiting office. Then there was the sacred principle of access. Jackson had been questioned concerning the theft of NO CANOEING signs from the bank of the River Lyon. Few things made a river more attractive than a landowner who didn't want it paddled and Dr Riddle was adamant about the Lyon. Leaked intelligence has it that Tayside Police kept the Jackson file with others labelled 'Urban Terrorist: Non-IRA'. Presumably it was felt that abseiling and kayaking would lead in short order to nail bombs and knee capping although a causal link is difficult to envisage.

His parents do not seem to have been too phased by his activities. They recalled: "We just laughed. He was obviously so earnest and well intentioned, and we had both been to university and were not unfamiliar with the kind of things that students can get up to. Indeed one of the high points of our memories of his college years was to open the *Glasgow Herald* – as it was then – and to see our son on the front page, in the presence of two policemen."

"One thing that always struck me as unusual about the way Andy campaigned on anything was his willingness to engage in debate," said David McGovern. "He always knew the other 'teams' at any given protest. For example, at the Timex dispute picket line, Andy knew all the local militant and socialist worker mob. He was able to explain to me the reasons for their disagreement with SNP policy. He took an active interest in their well-being after many of them were arrested at the demo. He certainly had socialist ideals and found affinity with their cause and also their level of commitment. He just had a slightly different cause and was going his own way."

Timex evokes very bitter memories in Dundee. The factory opened in 1946 and had been seen as part of a strategy for replacing Dundee's old declining industries with modern, clean, high tech employment. It diversified away from its original production of clocks and watches and in 1983 began production of Sir Clive Sinclair's ZX Spectrum computer. Unfortunately, the Spectrum was a short-lived games phenomenon and Sir Clive didn't come up with a replacement when the game moved on. In 1993 it was decided to invest in new products and to finance the investment by cutting into the benefits and conditions of the workforce. In January 340 workers, mostly women, went on strike and in February Timex sacked its entire workforce, including 17 who hadn't joined the strike, and tried to replace them with non-union labour. The 'scabs' were bussed daily through

ABOVE, TIMEX PICKET LINE. SPOT ANDY JUST LEFT OF CENTRE!
BELOW, ANDY INVITED ALEX SALMOND, LEADER OF THE
SCOTTISH NATIONAL PARTY, TO COMBINE A TALK TO STUDENTS AT
NORTHERN COLLEGE WITH A VISIT TO THE TIMEX PICKET LINE.

angry picket lines. Militant socialist activists appeared from London and Birmingham and vigorous confrontations with the police became routine. McGovern recalls being shocked by the way in which the police acted against the ringleaders for the most spurious reasons. Andy's tall figure was a regular feature on the picket line, shouting his protests at the police. McGovern remembers that when he and Andy persuaded Alex Salmond to come to Timex he spoke to the striking workers and carefully avoided the professional Trots and assorted state sponsored revolutionaries.

The early 1990s was a time of turmoil over the notorious Community Charge or Poll Tax. Local government had traditionally been part funded from the rates, a property based tax. Small families living in large, upmarket houses paid much more per head than several generations living together in one house on a council estate. This had always been a point of grievance with Conservative voters so Mrs Thatcher's administration abolished the rates and introduced a flat rate charge based on the number of adults living in the property. Castle dwelling widows were ecstatic but the change was far from universally popular. As a review of rateable values was due in Scotland the system was introduced there first, giving rise to accusations that Scotland was being used as a testing ground for new right wing policies. These suspicions were encouraged by proposals to build the Skye Bridge as a privately financed toll venture. The bridge eventually cost about £25 million to build. £33m were collected in tolls in nine years before the Scottish Executive bought it for an additional £27m. The early 1990s witnessed growing anger in Scotland and a feeling that the Conservative Government had been foisted on the Scots by voters in the South. The vigorous protests against the poll tax, the growth of Scottish nationalism and the campaign for a referendum on how Scotland should be governed all stemmed, at least in part, from this and Andy Jackson played a not inconspicuous part.

The most immediate response to the new tax was mass refusal to pay. According to Rodney Jameson, a student friend: "Andy's and Fozzy's favourite T-shirt was a Picture of a Rotweiler dog with the words 'Bailiffs, make my day' written on the front and 'Pay No Poll Tax' on the back. Andy was up to so much during this time it was hard to keep up, but I am sure that he did attend people's houses and disrupt sales, etc. We had a no pay policy in the house we were staying in. We kind of went along with the vibe Andy was putting out and it seemed to save a bit of cash too. Eventually I got a letter (in Stornoway) threatening me with court for non-payment, this was probably a standard letter that went out, but it was enough to make me bottle it and pay up. Andy however took a different approach. I doubt if he ever paid." To this day every council in Scotland has a significant backlog of uncollected tax from this era.

Various measures were taken against those who refused to pay, the most notorious of which were warrant sales. Armed with a court order secured by the council, bailiffs supported by the police would arrive to seize the personal effects of the defaulter whose possessions would later be sold to pay the tax. It was this that first brought Tommy Sheridan to prominence as he was frequently to the fore when angry crowds, screaming abuse, convened to obstruct the bailiffs. Sheridan spent four months in gaol for defying court orders relating to these protests. Andy Jackson for his part was frequently a vocal presence at poindings, when bailiffs attempted to remove TVs and microwaves from defaulters' homes. Like his housemates, he defiantly followed the "Can pay, won't pay" line. David McGovern gained a little respect for at least one of their opponents.

"We had gone to Whitfield High School in Dundee to protest at the Poll Tax. Lord James Douglas-Hamilton was there and came across to have a debate with those of us who had gone to throw their poll tax demand books at him! Fair play to the guy, he entered into a very well mannered, but vociferous debate with a 7ft skinny, SNP badge wearing ruffian. Unforgettable! I'd love a photo of that." Thatcher ignored the lesson from Scotland and introduced the tax south of the border, where it provoked the demonstrations and riots that contributed to her downfall.

Andy's time in tertiary education also coincided with the change from grants to student loans. When I was a student in Dundee in the late 1960s the generous state subsidised me to the extent of £1 per day. This was enough to cover the cost of living, fully catered for, in halls of residence. Other costs were met by a parental contribution and holiday income from construction or forestry labour. It was virtually unknown for students to have term-time jobs. They were, in any case, far too busy studying, debating, acting, singing, climbing hills, kayaking, partying, etc. They left university penniless but unencumbered by debt. Few students found Mrs Thatcher's proposed changes to a system based on loans backed up by part-time work in bars, supermarkets and sauna parlours attractive. Nor initially did the banks. The scheme looked like a non-starter, initially until the Royal Bank of Scotland agreed to back it and student life has never been the same since. For its contribution, The Royal Bank attracted the wrath of Andy Jackson and other likeminded individuals. Rodney Jameson now lives back home in Stornoway where the Atlantic, and the occasional jaunt to Morocco, provides most of the surf he needs. As one of the inmates of the notorious Jackson house and very close friend he recalls: "Andy took part in (or joint organised) a sit-in in the Royal Bank in Dundee, I wasn't there, but I think a pile of students went in to the bank, sat down and just refused to leave, you can picture it. Andy did all he could to make sure that the 'Anti Royal Bank of Scotland' vibe was in people's minds, in relation to any individuals thinking of opening accounts or taking out loans."

Like Timex the student loans campaign ultimately proved a lost cause. It takes the courage, and some would say the folly, of youth to take on the combined might of government and one of the worlds biggest and most dynamic banks. His campaign against damming burns to generate small amounts of green energy shows that he never lost the will to take on the big corporations for that in which he believed. It is said that "you can't win them all" and not all Andy's passions were lost causes. Take, for instance, the government of Scotland.

When the 1979 referendum on Scottish Devolution was held a narrow majority voted for home rule but the number fell short of the required 40% of the electorate. Scotland's unease with Thatcherism revived the idea. Andy favoured not just limited devolution but full blown independence within the European Union. In this, as with the poll tax, he was very much a child of his times. Thatcher's appeal to middle England simply didn't work north of the border where educated middle class people had deep reservations about socially divisive policies, described by Gordon Brown as "the politics of greed". Many Scots also felt that there was a democratic deficit, there was nothing they could do to influence the government through the ballot box and that demonstrations and protests were all that remained to them. Few were involved in as many as Andy Jackson. A theme that arises time and again when people talk about Andy is his inclusiveness. In the opinion of world tourist Andy England: "His popularity, from Kathmandu to Kinlochleven, was based on his unerring treatment of others as equals. Andy was no snob, and wore no blinkers. He was interested in what went on around him and had genuine warmth for other people. His big personality was a perfect match for his frame."

The election of the Labour Government in 1997 and the subsequent referendum on Scottish Devolution led to the re-opening of a Scottish Parliament in 1999. At the time of writing, with Alex Salmond heading a minority SNP administration, Andy might feel that Scotland is still going with his flow.

At the end of his student years Northern College had been so annoyed by him that it sought to deny him a degree. As an institution it had always valued compliance above passion and initiative in the young. After much fuss the college capitulated but Andy wasn't finished. His big (well elder) sister Claire remembers how annoyed her parents, Kate and Graeme, were that he boycotted his graduation ceremony: "They were both more than a little pissed off that he refused to attend because they were so proud and they wanted to see him get his certificate!" To this day there is a framed photograph on his parents' wall of Andy on graduation day holding somebody else's scroll!

Few would disagree with Claire when she said: "Andy had a personality that wasn't afraid to be different, always content to be his own person, even if that wasn't following the conventional route, and I think that is as much to do with Mum and Dad! Even as a child he was very content following his own thing – not afraid to be a bit different – oblivious to peer pressure, as witnessed by his unconventional 'fashion sense', indifference really to pop music etc. This I think displayed early signs of a man who would have strong principles and not be afraid to stick to them."

He was his parents' son. A decade and a half later the associates whom he dragged along with him in his campaigns are positive that he was motivated by principles and ideas, that he was not a teenage rebel without a cause flexing his muscles to assert his independence. To the end of his life he would continue to campaign on the issues that mattered to him. His concern for the environment was deep and genuine. Long before glass recycling became possible in the Highlands he and Bridget stored glass and then took it back to the Central Belt for re-cycling when they were going that way. He routinely picked up other people's litter and once returned home from the River Roy with an enormous gas cylinder, abandoned in a burn by road menders. He liked to recount walking along a street in Dunoon with a well built military gent when a half eaten packet of chips was heaved out of the window of a parked car, onto the pavement. With one deft movement the soldier scooped up the chips and returned them to their owners through the still open window. The guys inside looked at the size of the opposition and could scarcely manage a 'wee swearie'.

As the Bush and Blair double act began to wind up the machinery for the second invasion of Iraq, Andy was utterly unconvinced by the evidence that purported to show that Saddam Hussein possessed weapons of mass destruction. Believing that Iraqi oil resources were the only reason for intervention he persuaded others to join him on a protest march in Glasgow. He dismissed as a whitewash the finding of the Hutton Enquiry into the death of Dr Kelly, the UN weapons inspector quoted by the BBC as having said that the government had 'sexed up' an intelligence report. To date the media has treated us to a Woman of Mass Destruction (Claire Short whose eventual resignation was damaging to the Blair government), Whisky of Mass Destruction (when the CIA were found to be monitoring an Islay distillery in the belief that it was a chemical weapons plant) and Weapons of Mass Disappearance. No other form of WMD has been found and it looks as if the political judgment of Andy Jackson was far superior to that of the Prime Minister of the UK or the President of the United States of America!

WORK IS A FOUR LETTER WORD

When Andy went to Ardentinny in 1987 he intended to become a full time outdoor pursuits' instructor, a role in which he would have excelled. Nick Halls, the principal, persuaded him that he needed an alternative, fall back career. It was this advice that so disrupted the bureaucratic serenity of Northern College, Dundee, for three stormy years as he pursued a qualification in Community Education while simultaneously striving to put the world to rights.

During his student years Andy was sent on a placement to an outreach project with young people who were totally alienated from society and extremely unlikely to willingly present themselves at any youth club or other such organisation that might steer them in the direction of positive, constructive activity. Andy and his colleagues had no base other than the streets. They simply went into sink housing estates and tried to make contact with gangs of youths roaming the streets, get talking to them and try to lure them onto programmes in mountain biking, kayaking, camping and such like. The cynical might suggest that life had already dealt these unfortunates a bad enough hand without subjecting them to watersports with a youthful Andy Jackson. Community Education was not the only agency trying to make contact with these youths; the police frequently were as well. Within minutes of speaking to the youth workers the target clients might express their revulsion at the proposition that had been put to them by torching an abandoned council flat and then watch with interest and amusement the efforts of the fire brigade to control their handiwork and the attempts of the police to find out who had started the fire while protecting the fire brigade from attack by hostile natives. This really was working in bandit country. Frequently the outreach team knew exactly who had started the fire but the policy was not to tell the police as that would guarantee they would never get near the youth again. In the final analysis community education might prevent more fires than routine policing.

Those who worked with him agree that Andy had a remarkable talent for working with young people who displayed challenging behaviour. It is hard to imagine a greater contrast between Andy's own comfortable, constructive, secure, orderly middle class family background and the environment that spawned the disadvantaged, dysfunctional, alienated youth of what is probably Scotland's toughest city. Multiple deprivation was nothing new in Dundee in the 1990s. The city's rapid industrial growth in the mid-19th century depended heavily on immigration from Ireland. There was, of course, an overwhelming shortage of adequate housing with the result that the rougher parts of Dundee displayed the sort of squalor normally only associated with third world shanty towns. As a major centre of the textile industry there were always more jobs for women than for men. This tended to undermine male self esteem and led to a spiral of drunkenness, domestic violence, family breakdown and crime. The collapse of the whaling industry and the decline of jute didn't make matters easy. Beyond the confines of three or four good schools for the respectable middle classes Dundee is a very hard place to teach. The weak simply go to the wall. As in other tough places, some find reserves of determination and will power coupled with an ability to engage with their pupils that enables them to function and fulfil themselves. For a youth worker like Andy the learning curve would have been very, very steep yet Dundee gave him the opportunity to develop talents that hardened professionals recognized as exceptional. After qualifying he worked for some time on a mountain biking project with young people on the eastern fringes of the city.

Bridget maintains that, despite having very considerable talents, Andy never saw work as more than a means to an end. He worked to live. He didn't live to work. The Calvinist work ethic whereby we are defined by the work we do never got through to him. He was very reluctant to take on any work commitment that would prevent him going off on an extended kayak expedition. Being aware of his own value he bargained on being able to dictate his own terms and never saw any job as more than a temporary arrangement.

On returning from the World Tour in 1995 Andy and Bridget moved to Fort William. It wasn't intended that work would greatly interfere with kayaking and there was much talk of joining the State Sponsored Kayak Team. As there

CALIFORNIA SURFING DURING THE WORLD TOUR.

was still snow in these far off distant times Bid quickly got a job as a 'liftie' in the Aonach Mòr ski area, having first passed the training on how to smile and say "have a nice day" to customers. A vacancy in the local Community Education establishment quickly sucked Andy much deeper into the world of work than he had ever intended to go. Initially he was part time and temporary but before long he was full time, permanent and pensionable. Few people react so badly to a first pay slip showing a pension deduction. Assurances that he would grow old sooner than he might think and that a pension would be very useful, did little to console him. He was visibly angry and upset, like one who had just been mugged in the street, and contemplated resignation. Later he moved away from Community Education to a part time position as Access Officer with the Scottish Canoe Association, which did not carry nearly such a good pension provision. Few of us realize that we are going to get old and won't always be able to work, even if we want to. Young kayakers might do well to regard a pension as saving up for a long boating trip with pay. Andy never did grow old so perhaps this was something else about which he was right.

At first sight Olwyn MacDonald might seem an unlikely admirer of Andy Jackson. A Labour Councillor on the Highland Council she was many years his senior and not involved with outdoor sports, yet she was astute enough to see that Andy was a huge asset to the youth of her ward. She probably also realized that it would do her no harm as a councillor if local government services were seen to be effective and deliver benefits in her ward. Councillor Macdonald was forthright and open in her admiration of Andy as a youth worker based in the Caol Youth Centre.

Caol Housing Estate, lying between Fort William and the Caledonian Canal, was begun in the 1950s to meet a local demand for decent rented accommodation and also to house people moving into the area from Central Scotland to work in the Aluminium factory or in related employment. With a mix of different styles of housing, nestling under Ben Nevis, on the shores of Loch Linnhe, Caol is an attractive place to stay. It expanded rapidly with the establishment of a Pulp Mill at Corpach in the early 1960s. Caol's problems pale into insignificance beside those of housing estates in any European city yet beside its sensible, stable, socially responsible majority Caol has always had a minority of problem families whose difficulties attract attention out of all proportion to their numbers. Few of Lochaber's population are actually native to the area. Many have come to escape from something in Britain's urban wastelands and some have carried the problems of post industrial inner city Britain with them. When Her Majesties Inspectors of School reported on the area's main secondary school in the late 1970s they commented that it had more in common with a large central Scotland comprehensive than a Highland school. It was to these difficulties that Andy had to address his energies in the mid-nineties and Olwyn MacDonald's approval of him is a good indicator of the degree of success that he enjoyed.

Typically, Andy was not content with the available resources and moved mountains to have the community centre upgraded by the provision of a youth café with facilities that divert, entertain and amuse the youth of today. A friend and colleague, Mags Duncan said of him: "If there was a pocket to be picked Andy was in it for the kids in Caol. His natural exuberance and positive outlook drew people to him and they wanted to be like him. He was one of the best youth workers the Highlands ever had."

He had remarkably sensitive and delicate antennae for other people's feelings and a capacity to build them up and make them feel better about themselves. He was highly rated for his ability to handle kids who were being utterly bloody minded and determined to be difficult. Instead of banning trouble makers from the café for life he was much more inclined to impose a ban with a time limit, return being subject to the individual showing that he, or possibly she, had thought about the problem and how it could be avoided in the future. As in kayaking he seemed to be able to dictate that the world related to him on his terms.

Those who were around at the time recount tales of minibus journeys to Hampden to witness yet another Scotland football humiliation, camping trips, boating, skiing and mountain biking. There was a significant amount of healthy outdoor exercise to balance snooker and table football in the café.

Andy was well aware of the extent and value of his talents. He expected to be allowed unpaid leave from time to time for expeditions. He had little appetite for drawing up plans, mission statements and audits to please bureaucrats and officials nor did he relish being micro-managed. Things worked best when he had a line manager who was happy to do the paper work and attend the receptions to keep the suits happy and was willing to leave him to channel the energies of kids who might not always be angels.

By 2002 things were no longer running as smoothly as they once had. He was having trouble persuading his boss that keeping an extra-ordinary talent might demand out of the ordinary concessions, such as a bit of unpaid leave to go to Nepal. He was finding it hard to avoid his share of what he saw as pointless paperwork. A measure of frustration with some of the client group was also starting to emerge. He would complain that kids would appear enthusiastic about a trip but on the day would lack the motivation to get out of bed and go. This must have been difficult to deal with at a time when his own energy levels were low and he was struggling with a debilitating illness.

When Andy applied for the post of SCA Access Officer it was abundantly clear that he was ideally suited to the role and that Community Education would have to find somebody else to micro manage.

THE LONG ARMS TAKE SOME TIME OUT FROM WRANGLING YOUTHS.

LEFT, UPPER MODI
KHOLA, NEPAL
BELOW, THE WALK
IN TO THE BURI
GANDHAKI.

WORLD TOUR – NEPAL

Following the triumph of the 1993 world championships on the Occoee a plan was hatched for a long year out paddling the great rivers of the kayaking world. Andy later explained the origins of the trip in a magazine article printed in *Paddles*, February 1995.

Living the Gibber

Gibber vb. "To talk in an involuntary manner on a complex level in the present tense, about actions or events unlikely to happen. Often beginning...
"What if...", "Supposing..." or "Wouldn't it be good if..."

For those who still haven't got the idea, the following example may help.

"Wouldn't it be good to go boating in New Zealand?"
"Yeh, and you could paddle in Nepal on the way?"
"And in the States on the way home."
"Yeh, you could follow the best seasons all the way round the World."
"And every river would be at the perfect level."
"And we'd paddle the best boats."
"It would be awesome."

A CARRY ON THE ROOF OF THE WORLD.

And thus, on a cold day in Glencoe, our trip was born. Before we knew it, everything was falling into place. We were living the gibber.

As gibbered, first stop Nepal, arriving at the end of September in time to catch the high flows following the monsoon. We paddled a fair few rivers in our two months; well a total of 437 river kms to be exact. This included a good mixture of exploratory paddling and well known classic runs.

The journey down the Modi Khola from high in the Himalayas, a stone's throw from the Anapurna base-camp, through the deep mountain gorges of the Kali Gandaki and on past the jungle corridor to emerge in the great valley of the Trisuli, is one such guidebook classic. But first you have to get there. The journey starts from Pokhara, Nepal's second largest city, with a two hour bus ride. As the policeman shouted up to the bus rooftop "Permits, permits," we smiled with confidence of actually having paid our $5 for the relevant piece of paper. That is until Paul whispered: "I've left mine in Kathmandu." The following five minutes typified everything that we had come to know and love about Nepali bureaucracy. Smiling and saying "OK, OK" in our best Nepali accents, permits passed from person to person as kayakers climbed on and off the bus. Finally, the bemused policeman pronounced: "All is OK" and the last kayaker scrambled up the ladder onto the already moving bus. We were off.

Many of the best rivers in Nepal have no road to the put-in. Combining a pleasant trek with a superb river is great, except that most of us took up kayaking because we hated walking. As our potential porters feigned grief at the weight of the loaded kayaks, the price of a day's carry went up and up. We eventually conceded to 225 rupees a day. With a sly smile, the porters tied two boats together, carrying a double load for a double wage, and set off. It was all we could do to keep up.

Psyched for an epic, we were tempted by the guidebook description of a harder upper section, and were at once glad to be on the water. Steep boating and constant eddy scouting makes for rewarding paddling. The envisaged epic never materialised, but plenty of grade 5 did. At one particularly choked section of the river, Steve Woollett jumped out of his Hurricane to bank scout. "Hang on here guys, I'll check this out." After five minutes of jostling for position in the eddy, Steve returned. "You guys are definitely going to love this. It's the perfect rapid to run blind." As Steve's description of the carnage downstream unfolded, the line sounded even less probable, boofs, siphons, undercuts and strainers. "Its going to look really gnarly but it'll work like a dream." And he was right, well at least about the gnarly bit. A great day's paddling ended with Steve's kicking in the final hole, giving the rest of us a chance to laugh from the bank.

From here, the Modi Khola gives two days of good grade 4. Rapid follows rapid, with staggering views of snow capped Machapuchhre, standing at 23,000 feet. The river has an amazingly friendly nature, clear water and no nasty surprises.

There are no flat stretches and we headed downstream with the glee of a downhill skier.

Birethanti is a great place to eddy for the night. We stayed at the Riverside Lodge (where else?). Steep creekers should check out Rest Day Falls on the Burungdi Khola, the tributary which joins here. The final day of pleasant kayaking takes you down to the Kali Gandaki confluence. We opted to paddle with empty boats and Goose volunteered to carry the equipment the mile up to the bus. This decision, of course, had nothing to do with his broken rib courtesy of Rest Day Falls.

THE GREEN SLIME GUIDE NAMES THE TRIBUTARY AS THE BHURUNDI KHOLA AND GIVES THE THREE FALLS AS ABOUT 10M IN HEIGHT. JUST WHAT YOU NEED FOR A RELAXING DAY OFF.

[Rich] spotted a series of waterfalls on a small mountain stream across the valley. "Hope Andy Jackson doesn't see that," Goose joked. A further one and a half hours on the Modi Khola brought us to Birethanti. A moment's lack of concentration and Goose found himself being dragged off up a tributary. Sweating in the heat, Goose realized that he was past the point of no return; these were the waterfalls seen from across the valley. After a brief but cold epic deep in the gorge (which even the sun didn't dare to enter) the lads returned to the banana pancakes of touristville. Big smiles, shame about the broken ribs.

(Bridget Thomas, excerpt from *Canoeist*)

Setting off down the Kali Gandaki, we felt relaxed with the hardest rapids now behind us. As we drifted and enjoyed the scenery, we swung round the corner into the first major rapid, Geoff Parker taking the lead. He was soon being cartwheeled in the bottom hole; who said river racers don't make good rodeo paddlers?

That evening, laughing and reflecting on the day's paddling, we settled into the river life, pleased to be away from the hustle and bustle of the Anapurna circuit. Searching around for firewood, we attracted the attention of two young boys on the opposite bank. Realising what we were after, they disappeared from sight soon returning with armfuls of driftwood. "Dowra, dowra", they shouted, and we ferry glided over to gratefully receive their offering. Overjoyed just to have helped us they continued their work on the hillside, their high pitched singing drifting over to our campfire.

After a strangely restless night, we were joined for breakfast by two men from the nearest village. As we sat around the fire waiting for the porridge to brew, we chatted as best we could. "You slept here last night?" they asked with evident surprise. "Yes" we smiled, gesturing at our bivi-bags.

"I could not stay here." one replied, shivering. "If someone dies in our village, here we burn them. There are many ghosts." Glad that we hadn't met these men the night before, we exchanged glances around the fire, and rapidly changed the subject.

In total, it took four days to paddle the Kali Gandaki, time enough to appreciate the great scenery and occasional good rapid. On the last day, as the rapids intensified, we had a near death experience. Sitting beside the riverbank, a crowd of locals appeared bearing a stretcher, which was ceremoniously placed on a funeral pyre. Anxious to communicate to us what they were doing we were told in broken English "I am burning my friend".

"Yes," we replied, "you are having a barbecue". He nodded and smiled before adding, "My village is very because." It was our turn to nod and smile. As we left, the villagers took some time from watching the fire to wave us goodbye, and only Bridget noticed the feet sticking out of the woodpile. Taking out at Ramdi, we caught up with a great bunch of Irish paddlers and shared transport back to Pokhara. Ever heard the one about the Irishman who fell off the roof of the bus? Watch out for those low cables.

The Nepalese leg of the Gibber Trip could hardly have been better. The people we met and the places you see can only inspire more gibber.

"Wouldn't it be great to stay in Nepal for a whole year?"
"Yeh, and paddle monsoon flows."
"Yeh... but it's getting a little cold."
"Alright. How about Australia?"
"Nice one. Let's go."

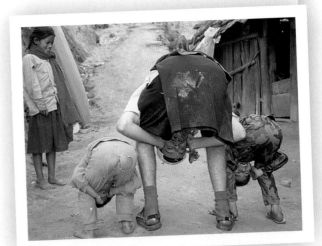

Whilst *Paddles* magazine described the group, which constituted Andy England (Goose), Andy Jackson and Bridget Thomas as Scottish paddlers, in reality, Jackson, who had been born in Wales and whose father was English was the only member of the group with a Scottish parent. He just speeded up the naturalization process a little for the other two.

Prijon kindly agreed to make boats available at each point along the way and demanded nothing in return other than product endorsement. HF provided buoyancy aids, helmets, paddles and throw bags and expected good exposure in magazine articles in return. Gear support also came from Andy's friend Roddy Webster whose gear company, Kogg, was still in its infancy. Other sponsors were Polaris, Playboater, Nookie and VauDe.

Andy had been to Nepal twice before. His first trip in 1991 with Callum Anderson and Mark Turnbull, organized and led by Chris Dickenson, aimed at a first descent of Mahakali but there wasn't enough water. His second trip, shortly afterwards, was as a replacement leader for an indisposed Chris on a commercial trip. His student flatmates arrived home one evening to find a note: "Back in two months. Gone to Nepal." It was the first they had heard of this. To be fair he had only been asked that morning.

The briefest examination of the World Tour magazine articles reveals how kayaking gear has moved on since that time. Most of the rivers were run in Hurricanes, 320cm long with a rockered hull for easy turning and a flat rear deck which opened up various play possibilities but which could play tricks in big whitewater. A cult boat for a while, the Hurricane was worlds away from either modern creeking or playboats. Nevertheless its plastic hull could survive levels of abuse that would have destroyed the glass fibre Everests in which the Mike Jones team ran the Dudh Kosi in 1976.

Chris Dickinson, Andy's former mentor from Ardentinny was also present in Nepal and recognised for the first time that his pupil had now clearly passed the old master's skill levels and had become a world class performer. Bridget's paddling had also made remarkable progress. Chris still remembers with horror the details of Andy's travelling light strategies. He constantly infested the one set of smelly hellies in which he crawled from sleeping bag into kayaking gear and back again. When asked if he intended to brush his teeth he replied that he didn't have a toothbrush and in any case he never brushed his teeth while on holiday. Cambridge girls are often very tough and adaptable and Bridget seems to have been able to live with this. Bridget insists she would have brushed his teeth with her brush should the need have arisen.

Chris recalls: "I joined him on the Tamur and tributary explorations. I left him to organise food as I was arriving late, literally the day before the trip over to the Tamur. I went with him, Bridget, and three of Andy's friends. He and Bid were paddling black Gamblers and a couple of his mates had Hurricanes. I was still in one of my Nepal Mountain Bats. The trip was successful for the paddling but a total disaster for food and logistics. Andy was hell bent on bargaining down the porters. Some abandoned us and we had to porter Bid's boat ourselves for a day. He was hell bent on knocking down the man who owned the crude porters' lodge we slept in, creating some bad feeling. The food we had was totally inadequate and cheap and it ran out. I spent a whole day hiking up to Tumlingtar just to buy some food. By end of this trip I waved them goodbye with some relief. I could see we were now a generation apart. In 1977 I had toured South and Central America for six months on $3 per day including travel. I did not want to go cheap any longer. Even less was I happy with the idea that we hassle poor Nepalis for a discount. The world tour they were headed for was not one I would have wanted at that time."

Bridget's recollection of this, on the other hand, is of finally agreeing a price for a kayak to be carried to the put-in only to see a man pick up two boats and head off upstream with a spring in his step. She is adamant they enjoyed good friendly relations with their porters. Goose, moreover, recalled that Andy would arrive in a Nepali village and be welcomed by people who remembered him passing through a couple of years before. In many ways their attitude is typical of young westerners when they encounter the bargaining culture of third world markets. All their competitive urges are aroused. They feel engaged in a game in which they will be ripped off if they don't front up to the vendor. Jackson also wrote: "The porters proved to be a valuable resource, the stars of the show. Get to know your porters; each man is more than a beast of burden. Their local knowledge was valuable from the translation of the names of tributaries (Majhwa Khola, said Mia, Love River) to the best way to reach the top." As the Majhwa Khola (grade 4/5) was probably a first descent they took the liberty of appropriately naming the rapids, First Love, G-spot, Pillow Talk and Bobbit's Rock. John Bobbit was an American whose most personal asset was sliced off by his often battered wife as he lay in a drunken sleep. This could be a warning of love gone wrong.

Exploratory paddling and understating his own achievements were two things that Andy did in equal measure. One of the more eventful of these exploratorions was on the Majhwa Khola. Andy later described the ensuing carnage in an article for *Canoeist*:

"Taking a brief afternoon break, we watched a traditional cremation on the far bank. Shortly before the half consumed body was committed to the water we got back in our gear to keep ahead of the remains. This was not to be. On the next rapid, whilst I was bank scouting, disaster struck. "How's he doing?" asked Bridget, straining to watch the line Goose had taken. "Not bad but he's in the hole... he's out... no, he's not... he's lost his blades... He's in the next hole... he's swimming. Go Go Go!" and the Sudden Happening Anti Near Disaster Immediate Evacuation Squad (Shandies) swung into action. "Help, help, no!" wailed Goose but the others wouldn't listen and ruthlessly forced him back into his waiting Gambler."

With daylight running out the rest of the team decided on a desperate portage round a section of the river complicated by a landslide while Andy set out to run it solo. Tension grew as the walkers waited at the bottom, and waited and then when hope had all but turned to despair the 'Prince of Darkness', emerged from the boulder strewn chaos left by the landslide. Comparatively little had been portaged. A defining Jackson moment. The final paragraph of *The Gibber* article tracked the next part of the Odyssey.

The Odyssey Continues…

"After a brief stop in Thailand we were soon enjoying the heat in Melbourne. Travelling to the Snowy Mountains we met Boris and Dave from Rapid Descents and were invited to join them on their next raft trip through the Murray Gates Gorge. This proved to be a fun day's paddle with lots of opportunities to laugh at guides and customers manoeuvring rafts in the tight whitewater. A high spot of our time in Australia was a descent of the Upper Snowy River. We were lucky to catch the river at a good level and it provided some great grade 4 water. All too soon it was time to hit the road, and we headed back to Melbourne well satisfied with our paddling in the High Country and excited to see what our next stop, New Zealand, would have to offer."

ABOVE, THE WORLD TOUR EMBLEM, EMBROIDERED ONTO T-SHIRTS IN KATHMANDU. RIGHT, BRIDGET AND ANDY IN THE BEST SEATS ON THE BUS.

TWO VIEWS OF THE PERTH RIVER, ONE OF ANDY'S FAVOURITES,
ON NEW ZEALAND'S RUGGED WEST COAST.

WORLD TOUR – NEW ZEALAND

By the time they got to New Zealand the team had been on the road for almost three months. This was a world tour on a shoestring. Bridget recalls: Andy and I spent £4,500 each on the world tour; that included flights and insurance (between £1,000 and £1,500 in total I think). We left the UK with very little money. We worked for about 5 weeks in NZ, Andy and Goose as building labourers while I sold discount cards. We also did the waterfall busking, some safety kayaking, some retrieval of lost kit, some house moving and other short term schemes. Despite their limited resources the world tourists do not seem to have compromised their principles much by working. *Canoeist* carried this report of the start of the New Zealand Odyssey.

In the land of the long white cloud

We nearly drove off the road as the radio crackled out an extreme weather warning, 250mm of rain forecast to fall overnight. Well, I'm not sure we got the full quarter of a metre but it sure rained and then it rained some more.

For a whitewater paddler the South Island's west coast is irresistible. Steep mountains rise straight from the sea, providing great river trips in a stunning setting, and there's no problem getting enough water. The team was in paddling overdrive, a ten day tour of rivers with some of New Zealand's leading kayakers responsible for exploring many of the area's great rivers. It was a case of sitting back and enjoying the ride as the locals were determined to show the visitors the best rivers on their patch.

When Bruce (chief guide) casually mentioned that he had booked a chopper to fly us to the next day's river we wondered if he realized just how tight a budget we were working on. Had he mistaken us for whitewater yuppies, jet-setting around the world from one great river to the next? We needn't have worried; hiring a helicopter in New Zealand is comparatively cheap, just as well as, with few roads and impenetrable bush, there aren't many other ways to get to the put-in and what a way to travel. As we stood at the side of the road the chopper suddenly appeared, flying low over the mountains. Ducking low to avoid checking out the spinning rotors, we quickly tied our boats to the machine and climbed aboard. Shouting over the noise of the engine, Bruce explained to the pilot where we wanted to put in and we were off. It's easy to underestimate the seriousness of a river trip as one scouts it at 90 mph from 300 feet up. "Don't worry," yelled Bruce in my ear, struggling to make himself heard over the din, "it won't be shallow when you get there." He was right; minutes later, as the chopper pilot put us down gently at the get-in, the River Taipo showed its true volume and hidden gradient. As the chopper disappeared we were left in the silence of the mountains with nearly 20km of grade 4 and 5 ahead of us.

"A classic," "gutsy," and "on the edge," the reaction of paddlers at the take-out said it all. For me it had been more 'on the edge' than others. Bridget had missed a critical boof move and was punished with a nasty head wound. Glad of our Gregson Pack, we patched her up and she was fit to continue, just as well as the chopper was long gone. Much impressed by the Taipo and the stitches in Bridget's chin, we teed up our next chopper and headed further along the coast to the Karamea River. In contrast with the Taipo, which was first paddled a few months ago, the Karamea is a well known classic. Several lengths of trips are possible and we opted to spend two days on the river starting at Karamea Bend. New Zealand is blessed with hundreds of back country huts providing basic accommodation in wilderness areas for hunters, trampers, fishermen and, of course, paddlers. We suspect this has less to do with sheltering from the weather and more to do with escaping the man-eating sandflies. These wee beasties can bite through clothing and leave one hopping from foot to foot without need for music. I promise I'll never curse the Scottish midge again. Staying in huts has the added advantage that one can travel light without carrying stoves, pots or bivi bags in boats, a big bonus on the more technical rapids.

Seventy years ago, a large earthquake in this area changed the riverbed of the Karamea forever. Huge landslides now block the river, creating several steep rapids for great paddling. The largest of these boulder-choked sections, the Roaring Lion, is a long grade 5 which roared briefly, taking another bite of Bridget's head. Oh, well, more steri strips, please. The lower section of the river contained more continuous rapids and had great play potential. Our hosts informed us that what we would know as a tail squirt they would call a whoopee and our suspicions about the effect on the brain of long term exposure to sandflies were confirmed.

During our time on the west coast we also paddled the Hokitika, Haast, Wanganui and Turnbull as well as some great new runs which I would love to mention but I am sworn to secrecy. A couple of important lessons learned (helicopter exhausts are hot and never pour petrol on a lighted stove, eh, Pete), we headed back to the relative civilization of Christchurch and our budding new careers with McDonald's.

Andy, Goose and Bridget also paddled with Phil Robinson and Pete Simpson. *Canoeist's* next report appeared in May 1995 and was written by Goose, who by then had time on his hands.

Kayak-busking and rodeo

"Bishops just move diagonally, yeh?"

"Think so. It's your go then, is it?"

"No, no, it's yours."

"Oh, right. What time is it?"

"Ten minutes since you last asked. Check."

"I'm bored." I declared.

"You'd better not be bored yet," scoffed Andy.

There was a long pause.

"It was a good idea, wasn't it?"

I offered, seeking comfort.

"Aye, well..."

1225 hrs – Call received. Maruia Falls.
Back injury. Code blue. Urgent.
1231 hrs – Ambulance despatched.
Helicopter on standby.
1244 hrs – Casualty located.
Suspected spinal fracture.

"I've got this great idea," Andy had said back in Christchurch, "we'll kayak-busk at Maruia Falls. It's the perfect spot, two car parks, loads of tourists, a viewing platform and a cleanish drop."

"Excellent," I'd enthused, "let's do it this weekend. We'll make up road signs, produce flyers, do the whole act;" and so it happened. Saturday morning saw Andy, Bridget and I standing in Nepali embroidered T-shirts plus matching kilts and hats in front of symbolically entwined Scottish and Kiwi flags, chatting to tourists and casually directing them to our subtle explanatory signs. We took turns to run the falls and got into the swing of

dealing with the public and raising enthusiasm whilst fighting off bloodlusting sandflies. We even had a local helper, Philip, to prevent the escape of non-paying spectators. Business was going well, despite aches and pains. Boofing was becoming a way of life and that night we sat in the ghostly light of a cloudy full moon, discussing the feasibility of developing the scam into a vocation.

On Sunday morning the rain started and our backs felt like cobbled streets in an earthquake. We warmed up and settled for different tactics, the pencil dive, surrendering to the flow, to avoid the impact of a ten metre boof.

Slap! "Hope he hurries up," slap "or the sandflies'll eat me alive," commented one of the more loyal spectators. It was Bridget's turn to be tour guide, her own scars still a talking point.

"Now for those of you with cameras, Goose will approach the fall just behind the rock in the middle. He'll then allow himself to go with the flow..." but I couldn't. Right on the lip, something instinctive switched me into boof mode. Sweep left, lift the knees. C-R-A-C-K! The sound was not of Hurricane meeting water but of vertebra T-7 meeting vertebra T-6.

The X-rays showed that T-7 came off worst, remoulding into a cheese-like wedge shape, whilst T-6 just lost some of its finer features. "Permanently," so spoke the cheery consultant, reminding me that a compressed vertebra is a broken back.

Despite an unlucky landing, I guess I was lucky. I got ten days in hospital, regaining mobility, and six weeks of easy living before a gentle restart to paddling. Lying in a comfy bed with the full benefits of Western technology to assist me, my mind wandered. There are worse places to injure yourself; what if it had been Nepal? Homemade stretchers, three days to be carried out by porters, poor medical facilities ... Or Scotland, the Topo inspired race for steepest not deepest? What if ... lying in the snow, frozen buckles, fighting off hypothermia? Back to Maruia Falls. What if ... no feeling, no movement; paralysis?

As record rainfalls drummed on the hospital windows, it did cross my mind, what if it's not worth it? In whitewater kayaking we get used to weighing potential thrills versus potential spills. It's good; it's healthy. It keeps us at the edge, keeps life exciting and just sometimes it catches us out.

Broken bones once more provided the perfect opportunity to take an administrative role (i.e. excuse not to paddle) at a rodeo, this time the Buller Whitewater Festival. Rodeo is still a relatively minor element of paddling in New Zealand, especially on the South Island where the focus is understandably on running rivers. Nonetheless, we got a showing of sixty or so entrants from as far afield as Germany, England, the States, Scotland and even the North Island.

Perhaps due to rodeo's infancy here, there was a notably relaxed and open-minded approach amongst the competitors. Based on a heats system, the atmosphere really was one of a cool day at the local playhole.

People who had never paddled rodeo before, relative beginners, rafters and even slalom paddlers, all entered to learn something fresh and to make the event happen. The results were superb with paddlers coming off the water beaming, not caring about their placings but looking forward to rodeoing again. The audience, largely non-paddlers, got involved with unified cries of *"Do something!"*, spurring the people on the water to do just that.

AJ SPLATS ON THE SHOTOVER, SOUTH ISLAND.

Under a blazing summer sky the heats got hot; Bridget was forced to a tiebreak with local Liz Blazey and had to pull out all the class she has to get her first place. It was, perhaps, in the women's class that most excitement was generated; Karen Armstrong, in a close third place, described rodeo as "better than sex"! With this in mind, the men were out to prove themselves and the finalists were almost impossible to separate. Andy Jackson was forced, yet again, into second place by Kiwi paddler and Nepal raft guide Mike Abbott, making impressive use of a temporarily vacated Hurricane. The open class had entrants in all sorts of craft from a lonely Topo through squirt and slalom boats to a boogie board. In the end, though, the Hurricane paddlers stormed to 1st, 2nd and 3rd in the open, and 1st and 3rd in the women's class.

Probably the only boat not to enter the rodeo was a rubber bus and that's only because they held their slalom, in fact the New Zealand national raft champs, at the same time. As well as adding to the entertainment (the public were invited to make up guided scratch teams) the rafts gave the paddlers something else to think about with an upstream gate placed tactically in the eddy for the rodeo wave. The rafters whoops and wheees gave all the warning necessary for kayakers to give way and the good humoured abusive exchanges just added to the audience's sense of harmony on the river.

The whole weekend was a great show, a a model for rodeo down under and good business for the Commercial Hotel, Murchison, the home of the whitewater party!

The boat-busking ploy seems to have impressed the hard as nails Kiwis. On 26th Jan The Nelson Evening Mail reported: "A group of globe-trotting Scottish kayakers conquered a patch of whitewater many would deem too dangerous when they rode the Maruia Falls recently.

Christchurch woman Marie Browne, on her way to a holiday in Golden Bay, watched Andy Jackson and two fellow kayakers tame the falls. Mrs Browne said the kayakers were from a party of five spending a year touring the world. Their trip had so far taken them through India, Nepal, Thailand and Australia and they planned to be in New Zealand until April, spending the next month in the South Island.

One of the kayakers had just had stitches removed from wounds suffered on two previous kayaking trips but still kayaked again that day.

Mrs Browne said crowds of people gathered to watch the kayakers as they accomplished something dangerous. If the kayakers had landed too close to the bottom of the fall they could have been sucked into the undertow."

Andy seems to have retained a soft spot for NZ. Near the take-out for the Affric, one of his Scottish firsts, there is a very imposing house with manicured lawns sweeping down to the river and a very bonglie (white settlerish) sign that promises "Trespassers will be flogged and sent to the colonies". Would you get to choose your destination? Andy was all for transportation to the land of the long white cloud while his landlord thought wistfully of the good old days in Kenya. The busking had been successfully trialed at the Falls of Shin in darkest Sutherland during his time as a Community Education student on placement in Tain. *Canoeist* carried the next installment, written by Andy and Bridget, in June 1995.

The far south

It was Sunday evening. The Buller Whitewater Festival had reached its dramatic climax, the party was over and most kayakers were heading home in time for work the following morning; most but not all. In a corner of the bar a small group of kayakers were pouring over a map, pausing only occasionally to order another jug of beer. Plans were laid and relaid, hashed and rehashed. We were a group of eight kayakers from four different nations with just two things in common. None of us had work on Monday and all of us had nothing better to do with life than spend the next month exploring the rivers of the far south of New Zealand. There were plenty of rivers to run and no shortage of ideas. We would embark on our mission tomorrow, tomorrow afternoon, that is; there was time for one last session in the rodeo playhole. Cash was running low and consequently we were almost out of chopper tickets; it was time to walk. Our first river, the Crooked, saw us grovelling in knee deep mud as we spent two and a half hours struggling up what excused itself for a path, our reward just an hour's good paddling. This experience fresh in our minds, we all reached deeper into our pockets and found the funds to fly in to our next river. The Perth is, after all, a 'classic'. We would have to rate it as the best river we paddled in New Zealand, definitely worth the money. If you're coming to New Zealand, don't miss out on this one; it's a whitewater paddler's dream. Several tributaries add to the flow and the river takes on a new character. Long big volume rapids littered with pourovers kept us from scampering from eddy to eddy. A few kilometres further the river was for the first time less than grade 4. There was just time to relax and take in the mountain scenery before entering the lower gorge. Sheer walled with river-wide holes, this gorge is the reason why you shouldn't run the Perth at high flows. Suddenly, flat water warned of the approaching waterfall and we were quickly on the bank trying to outstare the stopper at the foot of this four metre slab. Ollie announced he was going to give it a go and we quickly arranged some rescue cover. He tried for the left-hand line and just missed the ski jump pad but he still cleared the towback. Ollie looked relieved and the rest of us looked tense as we realized it was our turn to stop talking in ifs and buts and either run it or walk. Out middle going left was the next line to be tried as four more paddlers made the move. The fall is the last challenge in the gorge and the river enters its final stage, the play section. If you have any adrenalin left you will really enjoy the last few kilometres as there are some good playholes, surf waves and, best of all, the rock splat garden where you can park vertically against several enormous midstream boulders. We had a blast on this trip, six hours of grade 4/5 paddling, no portages and continuous whitewater in a superb mountain setting. One of the group had more of a blast than the others. Topo-man, whose name has been withheld for libel reasons, spent quite a while being recirculated in and out of his Topolino in the depths of a large pourover. Once rescued, he continued downstream, only to repeat the whole performance in an even bigger hole. The rest of the team would all like to thank Andy Hoitham for the entertainment.

On the road once more, we were soon in Queenstown, the home of New Zealand's action culture. Here you can pay to be scared in any number of ways from bungee jumping to jet boating. For us it was a welcome relief to chill out for a few days and enjoy some great playboating in the sunshine. We were even able to raise some extra beer money by hunting for paddles in a gorge below the most popularly rafted section on the Kawarau River, returning our pickings to rafting companies for a salvage fee of $5 apiece. The only frantic and stressful part of the day was the evening competition, a tent race. This ritual event, to see who could achieve a complete erection first, started many years ago in the American Midwest. Brought to NZ by our American contingent, Mike and Ollie, we were all keen to have a go. All the guys at VauDe will be pleased to hear that even in this top level international field we were often successful, being able to set up our home in less than 100 seconds.

Once again the nights were getting chilly and with autumn rapidly approaching in the Southern Hemisphere it was time to head up towards the equator and the warm waters of the North Island.

The articles the team wrote appeared in a variety of publications including *Canoeist, Paddler, American Whitewater, Canoe & Kayak* and in German in *Kanumagazin. Canoeist* in the UK, in particular, made a feature of these reports which quickly developed a following. Bridget thinks that it was probably through the world tour and these articles that Andy had his greatest influence on the world of kayaking. At a time when the gap year was starting to become fashionable young boaters realised that you could spend a long time away from home paddling class whitewater and experiencing the world. As we become more aware of the impact of international travel on the environment it is probably fair to claim that this way of doing things gives a better ratio of river miles to air miles than flying out to Uganda or Nepal for a few weeks a year. People who never met Andy say that they were inspired to travel the world and paddle its great rivers by the World Tour articles. At the time of writing (2007) Goose lives and teaches Geography in New Zealand which has also become home to Paul Currant, Dave and Heather Kwant, whose names occur from time to time in this narrative. Jackson rated the Perth River as one of his world favourite paddles.

RIGHT, THE CITROËN RAPID ON THE KAWARAU. THE RAFT COMPANIES ARE UNDERSTANDABLY NOT KEEN TO RUN THIS RAPID IN ORDER TO COLLECT RAFT PADDLES LOST EARLIER IN THE TRIP. PADDLES TEND TO GATHER IN THE EDDY BELOW, PROVIDING KAYAKERS WITH A READY SOURCE OF BEER TOKENS (BELOW).

LEFT, RODEO
RIDER ANDY
ENGLAND ENTERS
THE ARENA.
BELOW, AJ BOOFS
THE GRAFITTI
ROCK ON THE
KERN RIVER,
CALIFORNIA.

WORLD TOUR – NORTH AMERICA

The final leg of the World Tour was to North America. After two months in California they made their way home via Wyoming, Idaho, Montana, British Columbia and the Eastern USA, a major piece of travelling in its own right.

Canoeist, in August '95, documented not only the arrival of the world tour in the 'Land of the Free' but also an unusual amount of undignified swimming and the more usual encounters with darkness. The following narrative was mainly the work of Andy England although, as with all the World Tour articles, it was a bit of a committee effort with the others contributing ideas.

Southern California

On river right a large sign warned 'Portage, 100 yards'.

We remembered a quote from the guidebook, "Here, the wimps, punks and showboaters get theirs; only a real expert or a macho LA river dude would hope to survive the Royal Flush." For Andy this tipped the balance the wrong way. How apt, then, that halfway through the rapid he disappeared from sight under the first prominent undercut.

"It all seemed really sweet until the second hole, you know... before I knew it I'd hit involuntary splat mode. Looking at the sky... vertical... really horrible sensation as the boat slipped underwater and I was pinned. The force of the water just glued me to the front deck. Could I get out? Before I knew it I'd popped my deck and answered the question."

From the bank, Bridget and I watched with relief as Andy used his boat like a stepladder to reach the relative safety of a five metre slimy cliff.

We had arrived at the River Kern, southernmost of California's classic runs. With five months left of the World Tour, we'd devised a plan: spend a month in California working north, enjoying the Sierra Nevada snowmelt, followed by a month in each of Idaho and Wyoming and a couple in British Columbia.

The Kern itself is a wealth of whitewater 'whopportunities'; 90 miles of crashing waves and great playboating, interspersed with more than its fair share of grade 5 test pieces, the most famous of which is Salmon Falls. A powerful rapid leads to the falls itself where a guarding hole protects the critical chute.

It was a hole which proved to have my name on it. Surfing in the depths of the pourover, I was holding my own but not for long. This was no place for such games; there was a real risk of being surfed to the centre of the river and from there over the worst part of the falls. I made my decision.

"Bail!" I was laughing at myself at the time. "Bail! Kick off the boat and front crawl for the chute. That chute

was ugly! Tuck up the legs and go foetal... clatter off a few rocks and then down. I checked out the green room and then swam for the surface. Oh, well..."

I had lost a boot and gained a few bruises but was otherwise fine. Two down, one to go, and then it rained.

In America things are big. Big cars, big roads, big burgers, even the people are big. The very next day Bridget was to find out just how big the holes are. With a swollen flow of 6,000 cfs, a river-wide ledge was enough to complete our trio of OBEs (Out of Boat Experiences).

"I was spending large periods of time surfing the hole upside down; I'd get upright and dig for the end of the hole but I wasn't making progress and the loops just kept coming. Upside down again, I needed air; time for the grab loop. I surfaced on the foam pile and saw the rapid ahead then went deep. I kicked for the surface.

ANDY ON THE KERN.

One gulp. A rock slid past my vision and I went down again. Two more recircs and I began to feel the pattern. Haven't I seen that rock before? I tried to kick off it as I slid once more into the hole. No-one can get to me I thought as I went down for the fourth time. Relax. Try to save air. Down again. I didn't even know I was out until heard a voice and saw a kayak nearby."

The trio had been completed.

It's great to follow the guide but with Topolinos on the roof we had to do some steep creeking. The south fork of the Kaweah gave us the opportunity for which we were looking; what it lacks in volume it makes up for in gradient. We explored and ran a 2km section, great fun as long as we kept making the micro eddies. We left plenty still to run as we headed north for the rarely paddled San Joaquin.

The San Joaquin valley is sadly dominated by hydro dams but the river gods must have been smiling on us; we got good levels on runs which had been suffering drought for the last ten years.

One of the upper sections, Tied for First, has to be one of the highlights of the whole trip. It's a long eight hour day with an epic feel. To avoid disturbing deer in their migration season we started out boat hiking, then paddling two miles over a reservoir before rope lowering into the gorge. Buzzing through continuous grade 4, we stopped for a late lunch. Someone just had to look as his watch – 6 pm! "I don't suppose we could climb out of here?" Bridget asked, craning her neck to look up.

"What? That's 3,000 foot of loose granite."
"Has anyone got any matches? Bivi bags? No?"
"Oh, well..."

Spurred by the thought of spending a night in damp paddling kit, sharing a cave with bears and rattlers, the descent picked up pace. With no time to inspect, grade 4/5 water made for marginal boat scouting. We plunged through rapid after rapid, conscious that time was now against us. "At least it's a full moon," we joked, not wanting to accept our fate. As the twilight failed, we swung out of the gorge and recognized the last rapid. With the certainty of dry beds and hot food, we played away every last ounce of energy. What a blast! Everyone had a story of a desperate ferry or a must-make eddy overlooking disaster.

The same river gods must have also put a word in for us at dam control. The next day what had been a dry section, steeped in legend and unrun for years, was up and pumping. At Squaw's Leap the river enters a narrow grade 5 gorge. For those of you who have seen Soldier's Leap at Killiecrankie, we can assure you that cowboys must have been scarier than Jacobites!

Back to the present, we realized with a shock that our first month in California was drawing to a close. With generous helpings of both snow on the mountains and sun on the rivers, southern California had been keeping us busy. The team decision was unanimous; why drive north when we could happily paddle here? We've got time for another month in California. Plans, like rules, are made to be broken.

In September *Canoeist* continued the saga with a report of exciting stuff in California's Sierra Nevada. Bridget cannot remember who actually wrote this. It may well have been a team effort.

The Sierra Nevada

Good, solid dependable information is what a river runner needs from a guidebook and we were beginning to learn that our *Guide to the Best Whitewater in California* provided just that. An 'arduous three mile downhill hike' the guidebook had said and it meant it. Reaching the upper put-in for the North Fork of the American River requires descending 2,400 ft through dense forest and bushes of evil poison oak, and is the river worth the three hour struggle? You bet! The whitewater is excellent, your legs will recover and the itching and rash from the oak eases eventually. From the put-in at Tadpole Creek the river cuts a deep path through a spectacular canyon for thirty miles, making a great three day wilderness trip. The river is all action, grade 4/5 with whitewater for its entire length.

From the word "Go" the river had us working hard as we struggled with loaded boats in the technical water. Camping that night at what looked like an old gold miners' hangout, we were careful to hang all our food from a high tree branch. We had already seen one bear that day and if our supplies were raided it would be a long hungry paddle out from there.

On the river the next day we encountered some of the best rapids of the run. The river gradually builds, each rapid being more pushy than the one before, climaxing in a gorge called the Dream Gap, a stomping grade 5. Stopping for some lunch just below here, we disturbed a large rattlesnake which, after posing for photos, slipped away under a pile of rocks. We all had a wee peek inside our Hurricanes before taking to the water again.

Early in the afternoon we chose a campsite amidst the pristine scenery and baked in the hot sun. High in the mountains the snow was melting, and as we cooked over the campfire we watched the river swelling in volume. Reassuring ourselves that this was part of a daily snowmelt pattern and that the river would be back to a manageable level by the morning, we finished up our hot chocolate and climbed into our sleeping bags by 9 pm, long past the team's bedtime.

The next morning we awoke with a shock. It was early, horribly early. Paul, our morning monitor, needed to be off the river that afternoon to arrange his flight home to New Zealand and, keen to make an early start, he had us up at the crack of dawn but as we rubbed the sleep out of our eyes there was worse to come. Yesterday's warm weather meant that a lot of snow was in a hurry to get to the ocean and the river was running high. Our ever faithful guidebook warned of a nasty river-wide hole which is difficult to portage or inspect at high flows.

As we packed gear into boats in the cool of the morning the team was looking tense. Sensing an epic, we were on our way before 8 am, paddling silently through the initial grade 3s and 4s of the day. As the gorge walls closed in around us the river picked up speed and we were soon together in a small eddy, an ominous horizon just downstream and overhanging cliff walls above. The rock climbing pitons and webbing hanging from a crack in the granite walls were not a good sign; we had arrived at the infamous Giant Gap Ledge. Our descent had come to a grinding halt, and nobody seemed keen to be probe and run the carnage below blind and our attempts to climb round and inspect were to no avail.

Things looked bad for Paul's flight. It was time for dodgy manoeuvre number 226. Clipping onto the in situ climbing tat, Andy was lowered into the current towards the drop. On the brink of destruction, scrambling at the cliff, he was able to claw his way onto a slimy ledge and get clear of the current. Thanks, HF, for the chest harness! From his vantage point, Andy was able to inspect the fall. There was good news and bad. The drop was a gnarly 5+, possibly not runnable at this level, but it was possible to portage from Andy's ledge. Quickly we set about the process of lining the boats down the rapid to the portage ledge and, one by one, everybody took turns at sliding down the rope in the alarmingly swift current. With a couple of nifty rope tricks we were able to retrieve all our gear and the portage was complete.

After the ledge there was plenty more grade 5 but, luckily, no more portages. The last ten miles to the take-out included Chamberlain Falls, a fast but straightforward shoot, and some great playholes. Carrying our boats to the car, we knew we had been on an excellent trip. If you're looking for adventure, this three day experience is a classic. You could easily take four days over the trip. In fact, depending on your personal fright factor, your desire to play and the water level, you may need them.

After the delights of California, the trail led to the mid-west. Andy England wrote the following article for *Canoeist*.

THERE'S NO WHITEWATER IN WYOMING

"Wyoming? Whadya wanna go there for? There's no whitewater in Wyoming."

The Californians weren't impressed with our next World Tour destination. This year, with some justification, California is staking its claim to be centre of the whitewater universe, as is Colorado, as is the Pacific Northwest. As we drove through the deserts of Nevada we began to doubt our inside information. Oli and Mike, friends made in New Zealand, had promised to "show us a thing or two" around Jackson, Wyoming.

We needn't have doubted them. The 600 cfs 'trickle' at the take-out meant two things, full face helmets and Topolinos. Black Rock Creek was described as 'a classic', 'scary', 'you have to do it once'. From the top the trickle looked like a torrent. We soon clipped our first rock. It was sharp; it grabbed at the plastic and got our attention. It spun us backwards and as we looked over our shoulders we saw a grade 4 rapid disappear through a river wide strainer. Adrenaline straightened us up, found us a micro eddy and picked us a line. We were at the bank, no time to sit and enjoy safety; eddies are a rare commodity. We jumped out of our boats, threw them up the bank and stayed to make sure the next person made the eddy. Phew! There was no danger of a concentration slip now.

As we snapped our spraydecks shut on the happy side of the first strainer we started to realise what we'd let ourselves in for.

Our kayaking senses tuned in. Our focus shifted from immediate river features to distant shapes and back to the middle distance, reading the river but always searching for that ominous horizontal line. We felt the river and manoeuvred by instinct yet we dared not trip up.

"Everything is out to get you" grinned Gregg, our local guide who specializes in this stuff. There are no set lines, no inspections; the river tries to dictate and we fought it out but the threat of strainers always called the shots.

Black Rock, like many of the other rivers in this part of the world, carves its way through forested volcanic bedrock, tearing at the banks to create steep, sharp, boulder blast rapids. The trees don't stand a chance; as the banks erode they collapse into the river and wash to the first likely pinning spot, usually an inch or so from where they landed. The result is exhilarating grade 5 creeking, steep, continuous and constantly threatening. Mick Hopkinson, who should be old and sensible enough to be elsewhere, sums up the style as 'retrospective boating; it's best enjoyed in the pub afterwards'.

That night we tested his theory. Sure enough, the rapids got bigger by the pint, the strainers more numerous by the measure and somehow we beer-talked ourselves into the next 'classic'.

Warm Springs Creek flows from the same headwaters as Black Rock and has the same characteristics; a steep, demanding, strainer-fest with some even more bizarre features. A grade 5 rapid, punching and boofing ledge holes, makes the perfect lead into a crucial roll gate under a walled-in strainer. At lower levels the next logjam has a kayaker sized gap just above a three metre fall! Run at a high flow, there is no gap. We needed to climb the cliff to the right, tentatively lower onto the top and choose a log. We had to choose well (downstream is a good start), balance (careful) as we got into our boats and then pick a launching pad and launch into the grade 4 water below.

It is a good six hour undertaking, many miles from roads, cutting through straight sided gorges. A ruined flume runs along the river, reminding us of the gradient; in the days of railroad expansion, logs destined to be sleepers would be slid from top to bottom unassisted.

It's a blessing that there are so many portages or much of the scenery would be sadly missed! Some, however, could not be missed if we tried; swinging round a corner, the whole river disappears under a cliff. As the whitewater tourists scrambled for eddies, our tour leaders smiled knowingly and kept moving. Getting a firm grip on our senses and flinging them out, we were led into the mouth of a great cave. As I eddied under the entrance arch, wondering what I was about to do to myself, warm water trickled down my face and neck. Fearing the worst, I looked up, expecting a practical joke, but no, Andy was looking at stalactites. A naturally heated spring leaks in through the cave roof, its deposits creating flowstone pools filled with hot water. Hot pools are a common and well used feature of this area but these may be the only ones with grade 5 kayak access. From the cave entrance on, though, the river mellows and the retrospective enjoyment kicks in.

The two days planned for Wyoming soon drifted into two weeks, epic 'classics' being spaced by daily playruns around Jackson. Rendezvous River Sports, the kayak store, gets suspiciously busy every night just before closing time. For an hour at least, the store is full of kayak bums, no-one buying anything. This is the Jackson kayakers' hangout, the place to meet boaters and see what's happening. The owners, Gregg and Aaron, have nothing better to do than check river levels and plan our trips for us; go there but remember, don't follow them down rapids and don't buy anything!

When they both suggested a Montana trip and both wussed out we should have been worried. Instead, we found ourselves back in our grocery getter family car, passing the Grand Tetons, looking wistfully out of the window at beautiful illegal Yellowstone rivers and cruising effortlessly over the Beartooth range. As we started the descent, Mike and Oli respectfully pointed to the valley for which we were heading. "The East Rosebud," they said with reverence; "three miles, just one rapid but it's a good run".

Back in separate cars, we were concerned; these guys have a reputation and it was a long way to come for one rapid. We drove for a while and drove up a dirt road. They stopped. "You might want to look at this bit." A tree lay across three quarters of the river, above it steep boulder carnage.

"What's the line?" we asked. They shrugged, indicating left of the log.

We drove on and up, another two miles to a lake. From the glimpses we got there seemed to be more than one rapid but Mike and Oli were no help. "We usually put in and paddle under that bridge" was all they had to say. It was a good start; eyebrows raised and hearts pumping, we looked at the foot of clearance and took the plunge. There was silence as we drifted into the first rapid.

"Nice," I thought, "dodge the holes, boof a drop or two". This carried on for a while and around every corner I expected a pool, a relent in the gradient. Instead, the pace picked up, the holes got bigger and the gradient steeper. I was aware of boaters ahead of me and knew some were behind. Occasionally I'd see a boat in a hole and have time to avoid it, to drop into a hole of my own. Boat scouting skills were being pushed to the limit, looking from the top of every wave, using holes to pause and plan a line. This was not the place to be upside down but there's always the unexpected.

Crashing wave, see the sky, reach out and screw up. Yes! Facing upstream, spin on the next wave crest, drop into a hole. Stabilise. Look downstream. More holes! An eddy, left. Work out, weave through pourovers, make a couple of crucial boofs. Sweep. Big bow rudder. A rest!

I wasn't alone in the eddy; in fact, I was reaching past Oli and clawing at tree roots. Oli's beard was wet and his eyes were bright. This was serious. Gasping for breath and laughing, we were loving it. I just managed to pant "control ... skin of my teeth ..." The beard nodded. Boats went past. Deep breaths. Back to the mêlée. How could we have a horizon line when it was so steep? Oh... now it was steep. A fluorescent yellow blade pointed left. The strainer! Boof boof boof; this would be a disastrous place to pin. Make the left, breathe again.

For three miles this process continued. It is one rapid, three miles of grade 4 and 5 moves being linked at the pace of a downhill skier. The room for error is minimal and the punishments are severe, the perfect ingredients for a Wyoming 'classic'. The whole area is full of such rivers, rarely or yet to be paddled, steep, fast and hugely buzzy. If you're in Jackson, ask Gregg or Aaron at the river store; they're not as green as they're cabbage looking. For those in the know, there is whitewater in Wyoming.

LEFT, GOOSE AND OLLIE COMPARE BEARDS.

ABOVE, ANDY ON THE ROSEBUD.

Needless to say, the fun and camaraderie of a rodeo in Idaho, potato capital of the New World, was too much to resist. This article was a team effort but the Jackson style of humour will be obvious to all who knew him.

Dirt-Wheelin' Stateside

America; the home of big cars, big people and whitewater rodeo. After celebrating the 4th of July with a bang, our terrible trio Goose, Andy and Bridget headed to Idaho and "The Payette White Water Round-Up". A chance to surf our arms off and check out the US playboating scene.

Our family station wagon, 'The Grocery Getter', stuttered into the car park and died just in time for us to watch the juniors ripping in the playhole in the under eighteens' event. If the car had been capable of moving, I think we would have left then. These guys weren't hot, they were on fire! There were almost forty young people in the junior event, most looked to be under thirteen, not eighteen, and retendos and cartwheels were the name of the game. Scary to think that it will be four years before the winner will be old enough to celebrate with a beer in his hand. Jaw dropping, Bridget watched one competitor's ride on the wave. "Check this guy out, he must be really young." "Oh, not really," another spectator commented, "he just looks young, he's actually twelve". The future had arrived. Discouraged, we retreated to the car and pretended to outfit our boats until they had gone.

At the playhole the next day (oops we forgot to go to the slalom), we had chance to check out the site. Two steep waves dropping into a boat length hole, sticky enough to pull retendos but not enough to be intimidating. It was a great site for linking moves. Long rides were possible on both waves and with a bit of control, you could hang onto the hole for several moves. As the sun shone, we spent our time queuing in the eddy, surfing in the hole and then queuing some more. The long line was a good chance to chat to other boaters, learn some new moves and learn new names for the ones we could already do. We learnt that a front retendo was actually a 'Whippet' unless you got kicked out of

the hole, in which case it was a 'Polish' and go to the back of the queue. A beyond vertical ender could be a 'McTwist', although if you were grinning inanely at the time, it suddenly became a 'McCheese'. Then going for a front retendo, catching the bow and flobbing in, is actually a 'Pretendo'. This turned out to be our team's favourite move, along with 'Dirtwheels', you know the ones, you've lined up the cartwheel and everything looks great, until the stem hits the green water and you eat it, big time. All too soon, the competition was underway and it was time to "strut your stuff or just get stuffed while strutting." There were intermediate and expert classes in both the men's and women's events. This worked really well as it let the top folks fight it out while still giving the majority of paddlers loads of time on the water and a chance to shine at their own level. In the expert categories, there were preliminaries and semis and the finals were head to head. A two minute head to head is a great way of getting the crowd going. Just turn up the music and let exhausted paddlers go for it under pressure. Ride of the day would have to go to Charlie Munzie who pulled a stylish cartwheel, dislocated his shoulder, put it back in and went on to the finals.

Although we competed in the Hurricanes, Andy getting a first place and Bridget and Goose third places – we couldn't resist keeping the crowd entertained with some terminal Topolino paddling. That is to say that everyone laughed at them. Well, what would Americans know about anything small?

By this stage in the Tour Bridget was beginning to experience something akin to battle fatigue. She had run too many hard rivers, taken too many beatings and had too many bruises and stitches. She would have liked Andy to have eased off on the pace of things and done something more relaxing but it was '95 and that was never going to happen. It wasn't exactly choosing between his girlfriend and boating but on this occasion Andy chose to carry on boating. In joining her parents touring BC and Alaska, Bid was definitely seeking time out from the front line action. Whilst Bridget spent time with her parents, Andy Jackson and Goose (Andy England) paddled in the Canadian wilderness with veterans Kevin England, Al Collis and Mike Bouris. *Canoeist* carried this account from Andy England:

The twilight zone

Surely I was having a nightmare. We seemed to have been driving for hours. It was broad daylight when we left the Chilko-Taseko junction, a perfectly good campsite, for the Taseko put-in.

"Do you know what mile the put-in's at?" shouted Mike over the din of clattering metal and roaring engine. "Sixty," came the return shout.

"Not far now then, we've just passed mile 15." As the statements were mentally reread the confusion cleared.

"Sixty, Mike, six zero." A look of anguish came over the driver's face. This was wilderness or close to it. Road maintenance consisted of clearing fallen trees; there were no traffic cones here.

We had gone north to the Chilcotin plateau. Known not for its mountain peaks but for its wild and untouched volcanic landscape, the area is a must for a paddlers' tour of BC. Chilko-Taseko junction, the usual take-out, is unmistakable; the glacial turquoise of the Chilcotin river splits into the opaque grey of the Taseko and the blue green crystal of the Chilko.

There had been a relaxed atmosphere as we bumped, slid and ground our way up the track to the Chilko put-in. Neither of these rivers is a grade 5 desperate yet every Canadian paddler we met insisted we experience them.

Early morning (early for us) saw us warming up and playing the easy upper stretches. A committed Topo paddler Al Collis got to grips with the edges, rails and new possibilities of a 'long directional monster', the Hurricane! A committed geologist, Kev England drifted along upside down, casually rolling up for a breath and an enthusiastic description of the rocks on the riverbed. It wasn't only rocks down there; August is salmon season and the Chilko was busy with them. We weren't the only ones interested in fish; we passed a brown bear dipping in eddies, her three cubs playing and occasionally pretending to pay attention to the lesson. Bald eagles eyed

us and the river from the trees, not just one or two but dozens. Ospreys, timidly aware of their lower status in the hunting hierarchy, flitted from tree to tree before making the killer sweep.

The Chilko, though, isn't just a float. A horizon line told us the action was hotting up. Bidwell Falls is a classic grade 3/4 rapid. Make the eddy, check the line. Thread to tongue through an otherwise riverwide hole then crash and bounce through big breaking waves to a good viewpoint at the bottom. As the valley sides steepen, so does the river. The notorious White Mile was waiting and we eagerly paddled towards it.

Sceptical as we were (the White Mile was named by rafters, famed for their enthusiastic exaggerations), this was no disappointment. The quality of the rapids, beautifully blended into a mile long chain, was incredible. Seams, creases, standing waves, exploding waves, holes, pourovers, even eddies, every whitewater feature can be found at some point yet the rapids are forgiving; the more dangerous features can be spotted from the tops of the standing waves with plenty of room to manoeuvre.

The odd glossy wave could be looked right into, blue-green light streaming through the crest whilst the riverbed flashed by the trough. We found ourselves zig-zagging between features, playing the holes and surfing the waves, simply to prolong the experience.

The adrenalin hit was over after the White Mile but the Chilko continued to amaze. Still high as kites, we drifted into Magic Canyon. The banks cliff up and close together but there are no rapids here. The river follows a narrow slot in huge lava slabs, fast, smooth and silent. The silence of the water fell on the paddlers, except for an occasional hoot or burst of laughter as rock splats and tail squirts made use of countless eddy lines.

All too soon the bedrock gave way to braided channels but the Chilko still wasn't done. A great playhole, sensitively in keeping with the surroundings, lay hidden by an island. Here the Topos shone, retaining effortlessly in the shallow water. With the junction just around the corner, it was the perfect way to end a magical day.

Unfortunately for us, somewhat in a hurry, the day was far from over. The aim was to be at the Taseko put-in for the morning for yet another long day at the office.

Asphalt has its place, and its place is on shuttle roads. On the Chilcotin plateau it is unheard of but rutted dirt roads reach miles and miles to one-horse towns and small Native American settlements. The rivers, though, are everyone's food and drink so the road must, at some stage, get back to the river, mustn't it? Sandwiched between two long river days, the shuttle *was* a nightmare.

It's a good job, then, that the rivers were a dream. In the warmth of early morning sun, we soon forgot the trauma of the night before. We looked downstream and put our backs into it; we had elected to do the 60km paddle in one day.

The Taseko, sediment rich and cloudy, does not attract as many hunters as the Chilko. A bear here, a bald eagle

there... our biggest danger was of becoming blasé. For a long time the Taseko is a float or, at least, should be. We blasted through on a mission, never surfing too long lest the others left us for bear fodder! We almost tripped over Taseko Falls, marked by an impressive horizon line and a large block in the middle of the river. Quality was the call of the day, rapids which looked impressive and felt powerful yet were really soft and fluffy, none requiring boat scouting. From Teseko Falls down, there is a long section of grade 3/4, full of playspots to suit everyone's taste. We forgot about time for a while and made the most of the whitewater gems we kept coming across.

By the time the river was braiding, we felt like little children on a long journey.

"How far is it?"
"Around the corner."
"What time is it?"
"We've got time..." and there we were. Ponderosa pine gave way to autumnal aspens and we crossed the jigsaw puzzle line of the Taseko-Chilko confluence, enough energy left for one last little leprechaun move.

Canadian wilderness paddling is addictive; we were hooked and this time we didn't even want tracks to intrude on our space. The Stein River was recommended, three days, no roads but a taxi service to the put-in. What? The taxi is a float plane, easily chartered in Whistler to land at Stein Lake, the source.

The clouds cleared just in time to view the first day's paddle as we touched down sixty miles from anywhere.

It was too late now to have forgotten anything although, as we climbed onto the lake's logjam, we were all going through a mental checklist. It was worth sitting for a while on that lake, taking in the seriousness and remoteness of the situation. With the sun out and the banks rich with berries, it felt good.

The first day was a Scottish paddler's homecoming, low volume pool-drop and smooth granite slabs. We revelled in it, introducing our Canadian friends to the Topo ethos. The weight in the boats was no problem and we left the first gorge with plenty of time to prepare a campsite. The preparation was needed, too, clearing dead wood to make space for bivi bags, building a fire to dry kit and hanging food way up a tree, safe from any wandering bears that might have a taste for trail mix. Hanging the bags was easy but try finding them again at midnight with the munchies!

The second day was to whitewater kayakers what an Olympic steeplechase must be to fell runners. A lot of ground had to be covered and the water was flat. The excitement came from carrying loaded boats over huge logjams, precariously balancing and tentatively testing every footstep. The quiet and the wild, though, stayed with us and it just became a different kind of challenge.

A disused Indian camp, wigwams still in place, reminded us that what was wilderness for us was home for some, Indian mythology and superstition is strong in the Stein valley. Rock paintings, now faint and discrete, decorate riverbank cliffs. Spirits of people long dead to our world are said to be still roaming and haunting the one hut in the valley.

We were all getting tired, all thinking about stopping when we came across the hut. It was perfect, a drying line, an axe, a store and even a nice checkered table cloth. It felt like home as we cooked, brewed and settled in for the evening's story telling. Perhaps it was just the smoke and the stories but there seemed to be more than six of us there. A bunch of spiritual cynics, we were all reduced to looking carefully in the shadows whenever we left the safety of the fire.

The ghosts had gone by daylight, leaving us to warm up and psych up for the biggest day. By the time it reaches its lower gorges the Stein has more than doubled in volume. The rapids become more bouldery and technical, sometimes spreading out to make playful grade 3, sometimes narrowing into committing slots. Occasionally, the rivers drops away steeply in a churning mass of whitewater but almost everything goes by boat scouting.

The Devil's Staircase, a suitably named grade V, is unmistakable. The whole river is choked by a rockslide; a narrow channel forces its way through, steep, bouldery and very fast. Drop in, currents from all angles, hold the line, make a micro eddy, break in hard, work right, over the wave crest, punch the hole, keep the nose down, pick a slot and boof the next hole. Far left and far right work well, too; follow the footpath or scramble down the rocks!

The rest of the day (and it was a long day) was still

superb, continuous whitewater. By the time we left the gorge we were in an ecstatic, mesmerized state. Perfect weather, perfect water levels and an awesome place, the Stein trip was a classic of its kind.

Rafted together, gibbering away, we drifted into the huge brown expanse of the Fraser River and were whisked off to the Lytton bar.

Canadian wilderness paddling is about pure river experiences, a paradise for boaters of all levels and persuasions. Nothing is spoiled and there is always the feeling of exploration yet everything we did was within a day's drive of Vancouver, which makes them probably the most accessible wild rivers we have from wee Britain.

Anyone who ever saw Jackson paddling without paddles on the Etive or in the Garry or Kinlochleven playholes would be impressed by his technique, one of his recognized rodeo strengths. On the Stein this skill was to prove useful, as Goose recalled: "The Stein is a multi-day fly-in trip in BC, Canada. We had met a guy called Mike Boris, who was enthusiastic and learning quickly, but was a step behind. We knew the Stein was steep so we took Topos, so hand paddles in places of split paddles (no 3-ways in those days).

The run was great, with stunning whitewater and beautiful scenery. At the start of the last day things got steeper, and Mike got in trouble. He had a swim and lost his paddle. He couldn't possibly hand paddle, so Andy did. His arms were so long it made little difference. We had an incident-free day from then on, and once we hit the big float-out we did just that."

Typically the record of the Stein as provided by the previous article is a very factual affair. It makes no mention of hand paddling. Jackson was a genuinely modest individual and probably would not have wanted it mentioned. It concentrates on distances, times and grades, log chokes and falls, camp sites and open huts to sleep in. The final article from the tour was written by Jackson himself and was published in *Canoeist* magazine.

ANDY HANDPADDLES THE STEIN

What a long strange trip it's been

In native Canadian, *skookum* means awesome and *chuck* is water. The name says it all; the water has to be seen to be believed. Twice a day, for reasons too complicated for river paddlers to understand, the waters of the Sechelt Inlet empty themselves into the Pacific Ocean. For a few minutes calm reigns at the Sechelt narrows before strange currents start to boil and the water returns to flood the inlet. As the water pours round Roland Point a small miracle occurs. Well, actually, on the largest tides it's quite a big miracle. For five hours a large playable surf wave waits to be shredded. In the course of the tide this feature changes from a glassy wave to a large hole and back again. It's a different wave every ride; in fact, in the first couple of hours of flow we could feel the wave grow underneath us. Downstream, several large holes and whirlpools waited to entertain us and sometimes it was a bit of a fight to make the safety of the eddy.

With the sun shining and seductively big tides for several days, we were inspired to pack our camping gear and base ourselves beside the wave. It proved to be a worthwhile decision. In the evenings we were treated to incredible sunsets and as night fell we swam and paddled in the dark waters, stirring up glowing phosphorescence, another one of nature's little wonders. One night, Goose and his brother Kev found out just how far the tide comes in. Sleeping on the beach, they awoke in the early morning to find their legs afloat in their bivi bags. Whoever said that Goretex doesn't work? As they beat a hasty retreat, Al Collis and I laughed from the safety of our slightly higher piece of beach and hoped that the tide wouldn't rise much further. We were also joined by three intrepid travellers from Devon and together we had almost enough boats to fill the wave and many a story for the campfire.

The wave opened the door to some exciting and different moves. Straight from the world of board surfing came bottom turns and off the lip moves. Multiple crossovers were also possible, making for some neat team rides; synchronized rodeo is here! A new one for the books was star gazing, a wacky form of stern surfing where the paddler leans way back and sees a topsy-turvy world of water rushing towards him. I guess we had to be there.

Washing the salt from our hair, we set off on our homeward journey. It was fun to drop in at the Gauley festival in the eastern United States. This annual paddling get together is a crazy cross between the Mike Jones Rally and Disney World and it represents all that is good and bad in the modern world of whitewater commercialism. Thousands of paddlers take the grade 3/4 Gauley River mob handed before descending on the evening trade show in search of the latest in glittery helmets and armchair whitewater action. The festival is a bit of a zoo but that's half the attraction. On the water there was hardly room to flip a raft but, believe me, there were plenty of rubber buses trying. We found the Gauley to be a beautiful river, a brilliant place to meet old paddling friends from all over the world and a great way to finish our trip.

Andy made a number of return visits to Canada, notably in 1996 for what was, probably, the fourth descent of the Homathko.

ABOVE, GOT A TOPO? YOU'RE INVITED TO THE
PARTY! TOPOLINO RALLY 1993, ALLT MHEURAN.
LEFT, AN AERIAL VIEW OF THE HOUSE,
'WHINKNOWE'. PHOTO ©AIR WINGS.
BELOW, HOUSEMATES AL COLLIS AND
AJ TREKKING UP A WEE BURN.

THE HOUSE

Playboating had a picture of a house in the Highlands said to be infested by a nest of kayakers where a night's kip could always be had for but a few beers. I recognised the house. I owned it. As I called Andy the phone was being cleaned by the steam coming out of my ears. "How many copies of *The Big Issue* do you think you can sell in Fort William in any given day in November? You are allowed three lodgers and a reasonable number of visits from genuine friends. Your lease doesn't say anything about running a bunkhouse and it can be ended with a months notice."

Reassurances and promises followed that the property was being looked after. Perhaps there had been a few too many visitors and this would be curtailed. "It is our home and we have a vested interest in it." The *Playboater* item was the editor's idea and hadn't been approved by the inmates. Situation diffused for the time being.

"You watch your house if you're letting it to Andy Jackson", said Roddy Webster, one of his closest friends who had known him for years. Chris Dickinson has tales of Andy's flat in Broughty Ferry that would make any landlord's blood run cold; subdivision of rooms to accommodate extra residents, rooms full of kayaks and levels of cleanliness that would make the London of the plague look positively sanitary. Dickinson stayed there once and in his opinion: "It was close to the dirtiest place I have ever stayed. The kitchen was unbelievable. Within five minutes of eating a dinner prepared in there I was actually violently and repeatedly sick."

I sometimes wondered how wise I had been in becoming Andy's landlord but more than once, on the summit of Ben Nevis, he looked across and pointed out Whinknowe, white in the distance. For a moment it looked as if he cared for the place.

I was working away from home when my mother died. I had no intention of selling the crazy old house set in ten acres of swamp which had been evolving somewhat chaotically since my family were kicked out of Glen Dessary in 1820 and relocated to Banavie. I hated doing it but I did what I had to. I split the property in two and rented one end to a variety of tenants while holding on to the old barn end for my own purposes. From 1990 onwards Andy and a number of his associates stayed there with me while we paddled Lochaber's rivers.

After the World Tour Andy and Bid had no major intentions of doing any form of sustained work. For the foreseeable future they expected to be on the government kayak team. About that time all the exciting things happening in kayaking were going on in the Highlands. If you're looking for rain and crazy wee burns in spate it's going to be best in the west. Andy knew this already and he knew that one place stands head and shoulders above them all in the dampness stakes. Like Chamonix, Briançon and Jackson's Hole, Fort William has become one of those towns whose whole personality and atmosphere has been taken over and shaped by the outdoor thing. The hills, the crags, the snow and the rivers are a magnet and sooner or later everybody who aspires to anything will find themselves in the Fort, looking for somewhere to stay; for the night, or the week, or maybe a bit longer. First it was the climbers and walkers. John Keats climbed Ben Nevis in 1818 and he wasn't the first. From the 1880s the trickle became a flood. All the big names of climbing have been regular visitors and most have left their names on the list of first ascentionists. Harold Raeburn, Bill Murray, Dr Bell, MacInnes, Patey, Brown, Whillans, Smith and Marshall; the list goes on and on. In the '60s and '70s canoes were rarely seen in Lochaber. The Spean Gorge and the Arkaig had yielded to glass fibre technology but with the exception of the Lochy, the rivers were all a bit too tight and rocky for the long fragile boats of the time. This all began to change in the early '80s with the introduction of Tupperware kayaks. Andy was no stranger to the sunshine capital of the golden west having regularly paddled there with Chris Dickinson in earlier years. Before long he was telling me that he intended to move to the Fort and needed somewhere to stay. How about the Barn? I had no intention of letting my Banavie bolthole to anybody but, as it happened, the other end of Whinknowe was being let to a chain smoking architect called Stan and he was short of lodgers.

Predictably Stan didn't like Andy having large numbers of his friends dossing at the weekends or whenever. It was agreed that he could park an old caravan nearby for their overnight accommodation. This arrangement was never really likely to work. Before too long Smokin' Stan, persecuted for his unhealthy habit, decided to quit and move to London to work as a stone mason. Few events better illustrate the occasionally ruthless streak in Jackson. From then on in the whole business was one of attempting to keep the arrangement roughly as I intended and preserving the property while not falling out with the inmates too often. The deal had to be constantly renegotiated and redefined.

In theory there were to be no more than four long term rent paying residents. Visitors, and how long they might stay, were a completely different matter. They could also come at funny times of day and night. Sheila and I, down for the weekend, were woken by a big van parking under our window. The door slammed, there was banging on our front window and a nasal north of England voice demanded "Let me in Jackson, you bastard". At this point our highly territorial beagle leapt from its bed and ran round the sitting room barking and pissing on the furniture. The voice outside observed "Ah didn't know he 'ad a fookin' dog." Eventually we agreed that there would be no parking at that end of the house and that an assortment of about fifteen kayaks, belonging to dear knows who, would move from under my window. Parking and traffic congestion on the ten acre site was always a problem. Eventually a friend with a JCB excavated a new parking lot but it was a little too far from the house (15m) and was contemptuously dismissed as "the wives' car park".

At the bottom of everything lay Andy's extreme gregariousness. He revelled in the company of others, could not get too much of it and apparently could never turn away a weary traveller, or ten, looking for a bed for the night. A group of sodden, midge chewed French Scouts, desperately searching for a campsite, were once accommodated in the caravan. Over the years many of the housemates moved on and set up home elsewhere with a partner, often remarking that they needed somewhere more private to stay. The open house attitude had something 'Peter Pannish' or student-like about it, that never really left him while others matured or simply got older and wanted a bit more peace and quiet. Whinknowe simply became a relocated version of Andy's student flat in Broughty Ferry.

The rationale behind the whole thing is probably summed up in an article on the World Tour for *Canoeist* in which Goose (Andy England) reflected on how hospitable and helpful people had been to them in Oz, NZ and other desirable destinations, most notably after he had broken his back! "We were supported all the way by local people, mostly boaters, advice, enthusiasm, shelter, guiding, transport, friendship ... think it hinges on a communal love of boating and all that comes with it, the beautiful places, the joy of the water, the action and the people. We all share this and it forms a bond. It was open to us and we made the most of it. The sad thing is that it is most noticeable in every country other than our own ... How often does your door open to strangers; how truly hospitable would you be, faced with a bunch of smelly, hungry paddlers from the other side of the world? When London gets too much for them, when Nottingham makes them sick, when it rains in Wales or snows in Scotland, when they are too skint to buy a guidebook or stay in hostels, think what they feel and do what you can." It has to be said that somebody who lives in an area that markets itself as the Outdoor Capital of the UK will probably get more visitors than a resident of Huddersfield.

Andy also loved parties where he came into his own, much as he did boating. The phone would ring. "Are you coming down this weekend?" "Not sure, why?" "We're having a party, would you like to come?" Only very occasionally was it suggested that I'd be better to stay in Tain. The parties weren't really structurally threatening events. Fleece clad folks would stand about, or perch on the clapped out furniture chatting, listening to music, dribbling red wine on the carpet or stepping in puddles of curry. Since all furniture of any value had long been removed from the premises this didn't matter too much. The only question about the carpets was whether the bin men would be willing to remove them or whether we would have to bury them secretly in a big pit on the croft. Special parties were part of the flavour of any place that Andy stayed. Christmas dinner and Burns night were occasions of good company and some would go so far as to say good food. At his best Andy could be extremely funny. It is notoriously difficult to pin down exactly what is amusing about a funny person but AJ had all the important elements in good measure; timing, self deprecation, a sense of the odd and the absurd. Talking of paragliders in Nepal who had taken to flying with big hawks that could be released at key moments to seek out thermals, he would mimic the way in which the birds craned their necks and a story that was interesting became hilarious. His humour wasn't always particularly politically correct. Bridget became involved in a women's mountain biking group whom he called the dykes on bikes. Having finally bought a home of their own he was asked if it had a dish washer. "Yes," came the instant reply. "But she hasn't come home from work yet." Of course he knew it was naughty but good humour is always at risk of being offensive to somebody. Heather Smith, Denise Marriot, Bridget

herself and a variety of other talented women kayakers would readily testify to the benefits they had derived from paddling with Andy and that, regardless of the jokes, he was no misogynist.

One young lady spending the night after a party at Whinknowe woke in a room full of strange light and became aware of an old woman in Victorian costume staring at her with clear disapproval. If I had to nominate a ghost for this haunting I'd go for my great-grand aunt, Mairi-Anna, whose husband, the Captain, added the upper storey to the house. He was a genial giant of a man but also an elder of the Free Kirk and perhaps some of the goings on were frowned upon in the spirit world. How would those who in life had known little but work, and for whom ideas of leisure were limited to the occasional dram, or reading the bible, have felt about those strange goings on within the walls they had built with their own hands? It was a lifestyle that must also have confused sections of the local community, more accustomed to the house in my parents' time, my father being a pillar of society and again a Kirk elder. Few events illustrate this better than Big Al's leaving party, an event that has passed from the realms of reality through fantasy to legend.

Al Colis, long term friend of the world tourist, paddler, piste patroller on Aonach Mòr and inmate of the house made the strange and inexplicable decision to leave Lochaber and go an work at Whistler, Canada. Morag Atkins, Ben Race runner, mountain biker and neighbour will probably never forget the event. Although she lives 250 metres away it seemed that the party was taking place in her own home. A definite party animal herself she wasn't sure which to resent the most, the noise or the fact she, and her partner, Spook, couldn't leave their children to be there.

Big Al eventually paid a brief return visit from Canada where he has developed a successful business as a movie stunt organiser. In an unorthodox version of health service tourism a sebaceous cyst on his head was removed in the kitchen at Whinknowe by a junior doctor, then learning his trade in the Belford. The identity of the young quack has, of course, to be kept secret lest s/he be struck off. Bridget was deeply impressed by her/his sense of responsibility in refusing to perform the op the previous night when s/he was 'well oiled'. Dave Kwant's video of the procedure later thrilled a party crowd at Bruce the Builder's. Clearly there were certain risks involved in going under the knife in Jackson's kitchen but probably much less chance of contracting MRSA or C. difficile.

My main objective, as landlord, was that the residents should stay where they were and continue paying their not inconsiderable rent. Should they leave I would face the inconvenience of cleaning the place up, finding more disposable furniture and new tenants. The house also provided endless paddling, climbing and ski-ing opportunities. There was always somebody around wanting to do something and usually they would be very good at it.

Often there were one off days that were scarcely likely to be repeated, such as the house ski mountaineering ascent of Beinn Bhan, nearby, 800m high and covered in piles of November snow with no base. First of all there was the excitement of getting everybody kitted out. Who can wear these boots? Will these skins go on Bridget's skis? Will these adaptors go into anybody's piste bindings? Can Big Al walk up and carry his snow board? Do you really need poles? And then off; driving up through the forest, climbing over the deer fence, skinning up over the fresh dry powder. None of the ski areas were working, hardly a cloud in the sky. Ben Nevis and its neighbours, big and bonny behind us. Some got blisters and fell by the wayside, most reached the top and discovered again what we already knew; a thinnish layer of unconsolidated snow on grass with big drifts here and there isn't exactly easy to ski. Even Andy, a powerful skier, struggled a bit. Some resorted to kick turns and long traverses. Back to the vans. Triumph. A day well spent.

An additional benefit of having Andy as a tenant was that he could be a very useful source of gear. Prijon, Eskimo and later System X continually bombarded him and Bridget with new boats. Some of these, such as the Topos, seemed to be renewed annually, others were simply new models that the company was trying to promote. Some of these craft, it has to be said, didn't really suit Andy's paddling style while others quickly became dated. If he was feeling guilty or threatened by a recent excess of sociability or parking on the daffodils it was comparatively easy to blackmail him into parting with last year's model for a very reasonable sum. In this manner I acquired, over the years, a new Diabalo, which was ideal for big rivers, a well used Topo, which wasn't really ideal for my style of paddling, and a Xeno, which probably wasn't ideal for anyone's style of paddling. Andy's boats were always in very good condition with few of the signs of abuse that could be expected from a clumsy intermediate paddler. He could paddle steep, tight creeks without wrecking his gear. Eskimo continued to provide boats long after Andy and Bid effectively dropped out of the rodeo circuit. They knew that somebody would give them boats and they would rather they were seen in Eskimo products.

You didn't need to be good to paddle with Andy. You just had to be there and be up for it. He'd go on the river with virtually anybody, just as long as there wasn't anything better on offer. This could lead to a certain uncertainty and unpredictability. We had plans to climb route 2 on the Carn Dearg Buttress on the Ben one Sunday in summer but there was nobody at the house all weekend until suddenly about 2.30 in the afternoon Andy appeared. Rock climbing was Andy's third, or perhaps fourth outdoor pleasure and probably his weakest since he didn't do it very often. Despite this he had done some good things like Swastika on the Etive Slabs and a traverse of the complete Skye Cuillin ridge, including Blaven. Nowhere is the ridge very difficult but the whole is greater than the sum of the parts. The main ridge is only about seven miles long but it involves 13,000 feet of ascent. The climber never gets to walk, it is scrambling all the way and there isn't time to rope up, except for the most difficult bits. As tiredness starts to kick in the constant exposure has its effect and things that would normally seem easy to an experienced rock climber can become a lot harder and seem much more life threatening. Andy went to do the ridge with Dominic Serrami, but Dominic began to worry about his wife, who was about to give birth and left Andy to do it solo. Complete the traverse of the main ridge and you can consider yourself a mountaineer. Andy did the traverse from North to South, perhaps nobody told him that it's easier in the other direction, and arrived at the finish in a near delirious state.

Andy happily soloed Tower Ridge on the Ben where he was familiar with most of the other classic routes and easy winter gullies. Route 2 comes into the classics category. Graded as Severe it winds its way amiably up and across the biggest chunk of steep rock on the hill, traversing across or above the lines of the Ben's classic hard routes, Sassenach, Centurion, The Bat, etc. It places few demands on the climber's skills but does require a good head for heights. It was after three o-clock when we left the Distillery and headed up Allt a' Mhuillin on a warm, dry windless high summer day. I hadn't been on the climb for over twenty years and was pleased to find that modern protection had made it less intimidating. It was an odd experience to be doing something with Andy where he wasn't looking after me and telling me what I needed to do. After an easy climb up the left hand edge of the buttress the route makes a rising traverse to the right hand edge across steepish and occasionally greasy slabs. Relaxing on top of the buttress we admired the great cliffs of Britain's biggest Ben and looked across the Great Glen to the house that, in a funny way, seemed as important to Andy as it did to me. It was getting late when we got to the Allt a' Mhuillin dam, hot and sweaty. For the only time in a 14 year acquaintance did I see Andy Jackson swim in a river.

At the end of a summer day they'd often have a BBQ, look over at the Ben and drink cheap Belgian beer until the midges became far too affectionate and drove them indoors.

"Can we have a shower put in?"

"What's wrong with the canal? Besides you've got a bath."

(The bath was unusually short and Andy was unusually long.)

"Showers are better when there's lots of people. We get queues for the bath."

"Try becoming a recluse."

In many ways the old place wasn't ideal for them. Andy was 6ft 7inches tall. The back door is 5ft 10 inches high. Many of the other doors aren't much higher. Although there is enough headroom in the ground floor rooms, the bedroom where Andy and Bridget slept has a ceiling height of 6ft 4in, fine for 5ft 4in Bid. For a tall man to live in this situation for six years without sustaining serious head injuries shows remarkable spatial awareness, perhaps one of the factors that made him such a great boater.

Even before I decided to pack in working and go home to Banavie I began to suggest to my tenants that it would be a good idea for them to own their own home, an act of true altruism. Eventually they found themselves a nice little place. I even repaid most of the deposit, but only after the caravan was dragged away. Out went the AGA, the carpets, all the furniture, the bath and both staircases, but that's another story. Two showers and a standard bath were installed. Andy arrived from time to time to walk our dog and protest at the damage we had done to the house.

ANDY CLOWNING AROUND ON
ARDVERIKIE WALL, BINNEAN SHUAS.

Andy and Bid's new home was over at the other side of the Glen. Although called *Donarchie*, *Houston* or *Mission Control* would have been far better as boaters, paraglider pilots and skiers continued to converge on it in search of inspiration, a good day out or just a cup of tea. He continued to harbour useful lodgers to the very end. Bridget lives much more quietly than before. She often has friends to stay but only one occasional lodger. For my part, Banavie has no ghosts whom I have cause to fear.

ABOVE, ANDY TAKES OFF
FROM AONACH MÒR.
LEFT, ANDY ON THE ORCHY.
BOTTOM, SKIING LOCALLY
ON THE NEVIS RANGE (ON
AONACH MÒR)

THE HOME FRONT

Andy Jackson made the first descent of somewhere between fifty and seventy-four of the rivers listed in the 2nd edition of the *Scottish Whitewater* guide. It is more difficult to attribute first descents in kayaking than first ascents in mountaineering as boaters have never seen much need to record such achievements. It is generally impossible to be sure who ran a river first or how much of it was actually paddled.

Just below the new concrete bridge at Amat on Sutherland's River Carron lies an intimidating feature called Granny's Hole. Water pours through a narrow gap on river right and drops about 2m into a surging kettle hole, all but surrounded by overhanging black rock. Informed opinion is that an attempt to run this drop, other than at low flow, could only be survived by way of a well organized roped rescue. When the 19-year-old Jackson arrived at this feature it was late summer and it hadn't rained for weeks. The grade 4 chicken chute on river right looked horribly narrow and twisting, tight even for a mountain bat. Sensing his disappointment at the state of the river the local boaters who had brought him there led him to the drop that they had never seriously considered running. Andy and his companion, Dominic Serrami, took a long time to size it up, tossing bits of wood into the back of the re-circulating hole to see if they flushed out. The locals noticed how intense they were and how they focused on the feature. It was agreed that Dominic would run it first. He pencilled the drop, went deep and flipped. Normally a reliable roller, he failed to make a credible attempt to roll and exited his boat with speed, agility and obvious relief. Andy followed with his trademark boof, a flat landing and a relaxed clean exit from the chasm. It was the first time I had ever seen him paddle. As the evening progressed he ran two other drops that were only rumoured to have been run.

Exploratory paddling was what Andy was about. Paul Currant thinks that: "he paddled and explored many more rivers and burns in Scotland than anyone else will probably ever do". Andy Burton, an old friend and flat mate of Andy, was thoroughly acquainted with the groundwork of Jackson's exploration: "I spent many nights pouring over maps with him looking at possible runs, assessing the gradient and catchments before walking them on dry days then going back for a run in the wet. Andy had a book of rivers in which everything was recorded, possible runs in different areas, runs completed with everything documented and then there was the well sought after map that became the envy of every adventurous exploration boater in Scotland; there were a select few that were given the key to the coveted colour coded map of dreams and first descents still to be done or rivers to be looked at." His maps had acquired, for paddlers, some of the mystique that once belonged to Dr Tom Patey's black book of unclimbed crags and potential climbs. In kayaking, as in climbing, it is always hardest for the pioneer. One can never be quite certain of exactly how difficult a new challenge will be or if there are hidden problems. Andy Jackson burst on the Scottish paddling scene at a time when the new plastic boats were getting shorter and shorter, and rivers that would have chewed up and spat out older kayaks could now be considered. In *Games Climbers Play* Lito Tejeda-Flores maintained that advances in climbing gear enabled climbers to do harder and harder routes while keeping the same element of risk. Victorian climbers with hob nailed boots and hemp ropes were at no less risk on a 'Severe' than modern tigers with sticky rubber boots, kernmantel ropes and loads of protection on cutting edge 'Extremes'. Calculation of margins of risk was something at which Andy clearly excelled. He was able to use the new gear to push the frontiers of Scottish kayaking possibilities a long, long way.

Nobody in this era provided more answers to the old question, "Will it go?"

In kayaking he occupies a niche comparable to Harold Raeburn, Tom Patey or perhaps more appropriately Robin Smith in climbing. Shaun Baker reckons that tight, steep, knarly Scottish burns were Andy's forte. If he really did like to keep within his comfort zone these, perhaps, did not pose such a serious threat to him. If things go wrong, it is argued, you might get bashed about a bit by the rocks, well perhaps quite a lot, but you won't be endlessly recirculated below some awesome Niagara. Which, it might be asked, is preferable; drowning or spinal injury?

In climbing, kayaking, steep slope skiing and other sports with an element of risk the biggest advances are usually made by people, often keen to earn a reputation, who are willing to push the boat out a bit and accept bigger risks. Shaun Baker, and to an extent Paul Currant, would probably agree with Olaf Obsommer that: "he was not the boy for the super hard stuff." Andy achieved what he did by exceptionally high skill levels and an exceptional awareness of what the river was doing. Currant thought that: "Sometimes it seemed as though he had an extra sense of the river and its dangers". Callum Anderson feels that his ability to stay calm and calculating was a major asset in sharp-end boating. His personal preference was to stay alive and carry on boating. One should not, however, understate the element of risk in his exploratory kayaking.

On the first descent of the Affric three huge falls were portaged, one of which has subsequently been run. Huge amounts of water pouring over Dog Falls raised the question of recirculation under a fall where steep rocky banks would render bank rescue an academic possibility. There was also uncertainty onto what all that water was pouring. Farther downstream was Madness, probably the feature marked as Badger Falls on the map. About 50 metres above Madness is The Edge of Madness, a "tempting 3m drop, which is as fun as it looks". Andy paddled this closely followed by Duncan Ostler, a strong and talented boater with a bomb proof roll. It is pointless to speculate as to why his roll deserted him on this occasion but as his boat went over the first of the big drops Duncan reached the eddy on the lip, swimming strongly. When he took part in the second descent a couple of days later his Topo had a big bash pushed out of the front end, the grab loop was still missing and nobody paddled the Edge of Madness. Nine years later, in 2005, Madness received what is probably its only descent to date by Tom Brown, who recounts with enthusiasm how, as a teenager, he had found contact with Jackson inspirational.

The Pattack on the Spean/Spey watershed offers a fine intermediate run. Most people put in below the big falls. In the early '90s these were the subject of a sensational trial. A young man encouraged his newly wed wife to get into an inflatable with him, above the falls. He then jumped out and she died. Although it was discovered that he had just taken out substantial insurance on her life a not proven verdict was returned. From a kayaking perspective the main problem with this 10m drop is the lack of depth at the base and being stuffed against the wall at the bottom if you run it on the left. In high flow these problems may be overcome by running it on the right. Andy was rather reluctant to paddle the Pattack because it didn't have a lot to offer him other than the fall and he knew he would feel that he would have to paddle it again if he went back. This wasn't to maintain his reputation; rather it arose from a reluctance to back away from a challenge. Such is the burden of being a top man!

Jackson had a reputation for pushing not only his own limits but for getting others to push theirs. Andy Burton remembers: "... his lust for life and the outdoors and (that) he had the ability to talk most people into doing the most ridiculous of stunts that you never thought possible or would never have thought of doing yourself. He would also manage to instil an amazing amount of confidence in you and convince you that you were capable of doing just about anything and remind you of how good you would feel about it later. He was also the king of the 'sandbag' and I would sometimes find myself cursing him when sat above some ridiculous rapid in the dark miles from nowhere as he had convinced you that there was more than enough time for that last epic of the day or that the slope was fine, not going to avalanche and was not as steep as it looked and the walk-out was not going to be that bad and the fresh tracks would be worth it!" He usually rated people just a little higher than they rated themselves but would take no for an answer. Neil Farmer knew him as: "Someone that you could rely on. Someone who, when I was walking round the big fall on the Etive, said "good for you", after making it look ridiculously easy, when so ill, he almost fell asleep above it!" Denise Marriot lived and paddled with Andy and Bridget on and off for three years. She thinks that: "He had guts but wasn't stupid, I think his lack of ego kept him and those that paddled with him alive."

Andy 'Goose' England recalled: "Another classic Andy funny would be the '93 Topo rally in Glen Etive. We had about twelve boaters on Allt Mheuran. Andy and I were egging each other on into the last chute, which we chased each other down so close we actually bumped one another just before take-off at the end. We rolled up together in the pool, and sat back laughing uncontrollably as everyone else fell off the drop in various states. There was also a very humorous period one Easter holiday, as other 'Granite Grannies' and I kept throwing ourselves down horrendous low volume slides. We often hurt ourselves, broke stacks of equipment, and all the time thought that Andy had done the runs before us so they must be okay! He hadn't, and thought they were stupid (which they were!)"

Not for nothing was the epithet 'Prince of Darkness' pinned on Jackson. Dave Kwant, who knew Andy from about 1998, can still laugh when he recounts setting out on the 3km walk in, for the probable first descent of the Allt Choimhlidh, as it was getting dark. Not everybody relishes paddling unknown grade 5 water in near darkness, with two to three kilometres of extra grade 4 to 5 after the confluence with the Cour. Kwant concurs with Olaf Obsommer in the opinion that Jackson preferred the steep and twisted to big, high flow rivers. When Dave first encountered Andy he was in his first year at Edinburgh University and lived in awe of the older paddler. He spent some time getting regularly stuffed trying to follow Jackson lines down rivers before coming to the conclusion that Andy liked to paddle really weird lines and that he was best to trust his own judgement and follow his own lines. Bridget is sceptical, but Kwant thinks that Jackson believed that Scotland was the world's ultimate paddling destination, an opinion that some might find odd in one who had travelled the world and regularly sampled its most sought after streams. Was this simply another manifestation of his patriotism or an expression of his preference for the type of steep technical burns that Scotland offers in abundance?

Many of Andy's firsts were accomplished in a purple Topo, a craft which despite its lack of centimetres still managed to weigh 19kg. While relatively few kayakers are willing to carry their boats any distance to get on or off a river the long access hike was a Jackson trademark. With Paul Currant he hiked up the climbers' footpath on Creag Meagaidh following the Allt Coire Ardair for a couple of kilometres. This is a burn that can only be paddled in serious spate conditions when there is no shortage of other rivers to choose from. It requires a serious addiction to exploration to carry a boat, sweating into your boating gear, up hill for 2km. The river appears in the *Scottish Whitewater* Guide and it would be fascinating to know of it has ever been repeated. Many rock climbs are recorded by their first ascentionist and then rarely if ever repeated since their main attraction was to record a first ascent. A number of Andy's rivers may come into this category. They held out the lure of exploration to him but now that they have been paddled how often will anybody want to carry a kayak for an hour or more up a hill, sweating in their boating gear, to paddle just another river.

Farther west along Loch Laggan lies Allt a' Chaorainn, known as Rough Burn to the linguistically challenged. Here two or three kilometres of wading through mud and forestry plantation gives a stimulating grade 3 to 5 run back though boulder fields and over slabs, a modern classic with enough reward to justify the initial energy investment.

A passing mention of Gleann Camgharaidh (pronounced 'camagarry'), a roadless, depopulated valley west end of Loch Arkaig was enough to initiate a one hour drive up a single width road and a paddle across the loch to the mouth of the river draining the glen. Andy walked about a kilometre up this beautifully wooded river, commenting that the fit and the keen could go farther, before being rewarded with a good run back culminating in a grade 5 drop, which he called grizzly, into the loch. Again this piece of exploration may be the only descent this river has ever had. Loch Arkaig kept pulling Andy back, right to the end of his life. The second edition of the guide book contains the addition of Allt Mhuic, (pronounced 'owlt voochk') The Pig Burn, which he ran with Callum Anderson in 2004. Spectacular pictures of the drops have guaranteed a steady flow of cars up the B8004, past Andy's former abode in Banavie to savour the pork.

THE ALLT MHUIC.

A characteristic Jackson first occurred just down the Loch from Allt Mhuic. The drive up to Loch Arkaig takes the visitor through Am Mile Dorcha, The Dark Mile, with all its Jacobite associations. Bonnie Prince Charlie, the Young Pretender, has one of his many caves here and one novel in DK Broster's Jacobite trilogy is named after it. As the narrow defile opens out you reach Caig Falls, used to great effect in Rob Roy. The bottom section of the falls have apparently been paddled but the upper tier, featuring a fall onto rocks above the final channel and drop still awaits adequate advances in protective clothing. The great epic occurred in the narrow, conifer screened defile above. Details of how this burn was first paddled in the winter of '92 have entered kayaking folklore. The day before the event the river was scouted on foot by Andies Jackson and Burton. That night in the Commando Bar in Spean drink loosened tongues and next morning a huge number of hopeful boaters assembled in the car park below the falls. Andy's normal style was to accept everybody else as an equal and not to assume leadership or demand recognition of his status as a world class performer. It was all the more alarming then, especially to those who knew him well, when he did assume leadership and start making suggestions that some might like to consider the pedestrian option. On this occasion he outlined the attractions of the river to the assembled multitude; sustained grade 4 to 5 paddling, big blind drops, steep gorge sides, difficulties with portages. The car park quickly emptied as some sought more sensible options leaving Roddy Webster, a former Scottish slalom champion, Mousey, known to his mother as Mark Turnbull, Mr Blobby, known to his girlfriends past and present as Andy Burton, Graeme Togwell, know with great originality as Toggie, and AJ, known to the police as Andrew Jackson. There were others but apparently nobody counted them in and nobody counted them out.

The guidebook write up does not seem designed to encourage repeat descents

"If I ever get out of this I'm going to kill you."

"Oh my God I need a shorter boat."

"Ouch."

"He just went down!" "Yeah, which way?"

This isn't !?!?!? canoeing"

"Remember the Alamo."

"Thump."

"Did anyone bring a climbing rope?"

"That was a nice drop, what's it doing on a river like this?"

"It's getting dark. How many have we lost?"

"How many did we start with?"

Legend has it that Roddy Webster ran a 30ft drop that day, which he had scouted from his boat.

Many would say that this has all the flavour of a true Jackson outing. Remarkably the second edition of the guide records that Allt Chia-aig has had several descents and even repeat visits; a real tribute to the determination of boaters not to be phased by reputation or apparent difficulty.

Andy would reluctantly have accepted the need to spell out exactly what the river was likely to offer. Paul Currant was impressed by Jackson: "... always getting his and the group's act together whether it was surviving in the wilderness or optimising a day's boating in Scotland. But he never seemed to be bossy... we all used to ask and look to him for 'advice' and direction. He was incredibly sure of himself in a humble way." Sometimes his assumption of leadership could have an unnerving effect. About a year before he died he found himself on the Upper Spean with four friends who were competent enough for that grade of river but perhaps a little in awe of the huge clouds of spray that arose from the base of dam as water roared from all six siphons and spilled over the top of the dam. The very fact that Andy assumed formal leadership of the group urged us not to be intimidated by the darkness and the spray and ordained an order for the group to follow him gave it added significance and menace. With the dam releasing a decent amount of water the main problem is a near river-wide stopper near the start. Putting in on river right, the conventional solution is to paddle across and outflank the stopper hard on river left, taking care not to get caught on any alder twigs sticking out of the torrent. This is normally fairly straightforward but a few years back people were sometimes tempted to sneak down the right at the start, perhaps fearing that short boats might be too slow to make it across above the stopper. This was the course that Andy elected to follow but no real chicken run existed that day. He was looped in a meaty stopper, in itself a most unusual event, especially as he was in a Salto. Denise Marriot flipped and Mark Laidlaw, alias Soup, went straight over his ex-girlfriend before she rolled up. Aussie Dave had a clean run but, nominated to bring up the rear, I embarked on the foolish and dangerous course of thinking for myself and began a seriously too late attempt to go to river left. This inevitably resulted in playing in the hole where nobody must go. It was comforting to know in advance that there are known survivors. Roddy Webster has experienced it full strength. An initial strategy of side surfing the remaining ten metres to river left seemed to be going well until the boat did a quite uncalled-for spin followed by a flip. I rolled up with the feeling of one who had been on the electric chair during a power cut, paddling furiously to elude the tow-back. Downstream Andy hovered with the group in an eddy, uncertain for once of his priorities. Could he leave the group to help me or did they need his support. Fortunately this issue resolved itself.

With the playhole behind, the river became a huge, rampaging wave train, with swirls, boils and enormous waves. Stoppers of any sort are few and far apart and easily avoided. Breakouts are little more than an academic possibility as the flooded river inundates the alder scrub on the bank. A mile below the dam respite can be taken on the downstream side of the railway bridge. After this the river gradually loses most of it power until it reaches the gorge at Inverlair where the water is forced through a narrow rocky channel producing grade 4 features that would be attractive were it not for the monstrous grade 6 homicidal fall that lurks at the end of the gorge. Most of the water pours over the right in a cascade of truly awesome pour. A side channel on river left goes over a couple of significant ledges before plunging some six metres over a steep slab into the heaving flood below. Aged 20, Andy described this as the chicken chute and said it was grade 3+. It looks like a chute for very plucky chickens but then it has to be remembered that Andy gave the same grade to the Etive, which others consider 4+ or 5. When he and Paul Currant made the first descent of this rarely run drop they did seem to focus with an intensity that belied the 3+ grading. He always had reservations about gradings, favouring the yes/no system. Yes, I'll run it. No, I'll walk.

It wasn't all exploratory paddling; there was more to Jackson than that. Bridget recalls that Kevin Danforth – who worked for the BCU, did a lot of judging at the early rodeos and selected, and was team manager for, the British team at the Ocoee in 1993 – said of Andy's performance at rodeos that: "he did well because of his hand paddling (which used to score double points for each move) and his cheeky grin". Even to those who struggle to remain upright for more than a couple of spins, it was a joy to watch him surfing the Garry or the Kinlochleven playhole with only his enormous hands and legendary long arms to impel the boat. If you daren't even dream of cartwheels it's incredible to see them done manually. Naturally an ability to hand roll in whitewater is helpful; leaving his paddles behind could spice up old favourites like the Etive. Comparatively few of us will happily embark on 3km of grade 4 and 5 paddling, complete with a 6m drop, empty handed save for some bath floats. His playboating skills commanded the respect of top-end performers like Paul Currant who has abiding memories of "watching him do effortless cartwheels in a Topolino in the Orchy playhole even when he was feeling like shit".

The whole business of playboating developed hugely during sixteen years of his kayaking life. In 1990, when he first took his brand new yellow Gatino to the Garry playhole, it consisted of surfing, side surfing, loops and pop-outs and not much else. The big challenge on the Garry was to side surf the Gatino, considered then to be an outrageously short boat, along the wave, turn

ABOVE, ANDY HAND
PADDLES THE TOPO ON HIS
WAY TO A DOUBLE SCORE
AT THE 1996 HURLEY
RODEO.
LEFT, AERIAL ON THE
GARRY IN THE AIRHEAD.

and come back again. Things had gone a little farther than this on the other side of the Atlantic and with shorter and shorter boats, such as the German made Topolino, coming on stream the repertoire of moves expanded quickly. Andy was extremely loyal to his main sponsor, Eskimo, and paddled a succession of boats which tracked the evolution of their playboat design from the Kendo, through the Quadro to the Xeno and the Nano. There was also an early attempt to produce a home grown playboat by heating deck sections of a Topo and squashing the ends. The lack of a flat, planing hull and clean edges limited the success of the experiment. Even his closest associates could never really understand how he managed to get the bottom half of his two metre frame into a Topo or a Nano, even allowing for the considerable modifications of footrest plates that took place! He also liked to have an out and out river running boat and paddled Hurricanes and Diabalos on a number of expeditions. Old time game hunters in Africa were fond of the expression 'use enough gun' and Jackson didn't subscribe to the theory that everything could be paddled in a short low-volume boat. German kayaks had the virtue of being very durable which is important on Highland rivers. He was enthusiastic about a proto-type Salto which Eskimo gave him to test, but finally he began to drift away from the German marque. System X, then the importer for Eskimo, began to import Liquid Logic kayaks with the result that he finally began shoe horning his great length into their playboats and paddling a Gus when the going was likely to get rough. Eskimo had never really managed to keep up with the design trends in playboating and finally other makers began to challenge their dominance of the market for river runners. Giving Andy gear was undoubtedly financially rewarding to his sponsors. Many of the items that he and the team were given quickly became fashionable kit in Scotland and beyond. Werner paddles and HF pfds were rarely seen here before they persuaded Jackson to use them. Although nobody would really accuse him of being opinionated he was willing to advance very strong views on other people's gear. Not long after I started to paddle with him he told me that he wouldn't use my helmet in a swimming pool. I respectfully demurred and bought a new one, which he accepted for about ten years before beginning a campaign for its replacement. After my first six-pipes paddle with him on the Upper Spean, circa 1992, he looked critically at my WW Shorty buoyancy aid and said: "Glad you didn't take a swim today. You'd drown in that thing." Fortunately his friend Roddy Webster, Mr Kogg, was on hand to sell me one of his big river vests which supported me well through many misadventures for the next fifteen years.

One of the most re-assuring things about paddling with Jackson was his ability to rescue where others would only think of their own survival. Neil Farmer admits that: "When running the right hand side of the Falls of Leny, for the first time, in medium water, I screwed up the line and was stuffed in the small eddy, under the central rock. I was recirced several times, beaten near to death and eventually swam. Even before I swam, when Andy had no chance of rescuing me, he came close and shouted encouragement! When I finally swam, with a cut that subsequently took four stitches and a swim under the rock, he pulled me to the side, smiled and encouraged me up the steep walls!"

There is a harmless looking stopper near the top end of the Morriston. Many years ago, according to legend, Callum Anderson, rated by some as Andy's equal or better, explored its possibilities as a playhole and in a dramatic case of role reversal found the hole playing with him. The women present recall that it mischievously removed the boxer shorts in which he was paddling, mercifully leaving his spray deck to partly preserve his modesty. After many years of paddling past without really noticing it I finally blundered into this feature, which clearly had lost none of its sense of fun as I immediately embarked on a series of spectacular cartwheels and loops. Each time I rolled up it sucked me back in and showed me a new trick. Upstream Bridget Thomas looked on with horror. Finally I surfaced a little farther downstream. Andy was sitting against the rock wall beside the hole, holding out his paddles and calling to me. Bewildered and confused, I dropped my own blades and lunged at his, which he generously released as soon as I was stable. In a classic stopper rescue he had pushed me out of the hole. Five metres downstream I encountered my own property floating and realised the implication of his kindness. I had left him paddle-less beside a munching hole on a grade 4+ rapid. But it didn't seem like a problem to him. He just hand surfed around a bit before heading downstream, to retrieve his blades from me, happily enjoying this most beautiful of Inverness-shire rivers.

Andy's strength and skill made him a formidable Topo Duo paddler. The first time I ever got in a Duo with Andy we began with a practice roll. His instructions to me were to set up and kick in when I felt him start to roll. Over we went and I began to push my paddle to the surface and then, bang, we were up. I doubt if I contributed anything to the roll but I could feel the power. Complete beginners were taken down grade 4 rivers or into the playhole on the Garry to spin effortlessly in the 3.7m-long duo. A large passenger who failed to follow the tilt left or tilt right instructions would occasionally cause a capsize. If he then panicked and swam, Andy would roll up on his own with a boat half full of water and rescue the swimmer. Dave Kwant firmly believes that his legendary long arms enabled him to do a variety of things that nobody else could achieve.

When Adrian Disney, then an instructor at the Loch Eil Outward Bound, broke his back cragging at Poll Dubh in Glen Nevis he became a regular duo companion. Since he was paralysed in the lower body he would sometimes flop forward or back at which point the man in the rear seat would grab his buoyancy aid and push him upright. Andy's empathy for others, especially those who faced personal difficulties, and his instinct to include rather than exclude, left him in the driving seat.

Adrian finally got a boat with a special back support that enables him to paddle solo. He has no hip movement and has limited tilt possibilities but he's out there boating and completed a major sea kayak journey on the west coast of Canada, an achievement that is part of Andy's legacy to kayak sport. Under the access section on the River Ailort in *Scottish Whitewater* Adrian wrote: "If like me you depend on a wheelchair, access is difficult for your paddling partner who has to carry you from the road and then go back to get the Topo-Duo. Otherwise it is a simple and short carry."

It is hard to imagine a sentence that could say more about the inclusive instincts of Andy Jackson. For a long time Andy kept fairly quiet about the new rivers he found. It wasn't so much that he didn't want to share them; he just didn't want to endure the access hassles with fishyfolk that might ensue if the masses arrived. Goose (Andy England) explained: "The guidebook was integrally wrapped up in the changing climate. I was with Andy on many occasions when people asked for a guide to be made, and was even asked for magazine articles to give away 'Andy's secrets'. But until the climate was right, and to be fair until the internet made info exchange inevitable, Andy and others held out on his wee gems. The publishing of the guidebook, and its style of production, was quite extraordinary at its time I think. It was also, for Andy, an immense gesture of sharing rather than claiming. The book itself was a remarkable team effort by Andy and Bid."

Chris Dickinson had been keen to write a guide but initially many paddlers were hostile, fearing that their favourite paddles would be mobbed. Indeed a number of Scottish boaters had come in for criticism for publishing magazine articles on Highland rivers. "Although the guidebook project started with me", Dickinson maintains, "I received little encouragement." Eventually the project was taken over by the SCA with Jackson and Thomas as editors.

There had, of course, been guidebooks before but until Mark Rainsley's online guide came along they simply hadn't kept up with the new style of boating. The decision to publish was partly one of 'go with the flow' and partly a gamble that if they came clean with hundreds of rivers they couldn't all be over-run with eager fresh faced boaters. The exercise began with asking kayakers with knowledge of particular rivers to submit a description. These came back in a wide variety of styles and with numerous idiosyncrasies, some of which were really quite funny. Since editing these to a standard format would have been a huge and difficult task it was decided to attribute them to the culprits who had written them in the first place. The book, *Scottish Whitewater* (Pesda Press), sold well and went into a second edition partly because it met a need but also because just about everybody who paddled in Scotland had contributed a river or a photo or had been immortalised in one. There had never been anything quite like it before. It established a new style that others would adopt, gave Scottish paddlers a sense of ownership of the book and carried forward the ethos of inclusiveness that has always been an attractive aspect of paddling North of the Border.

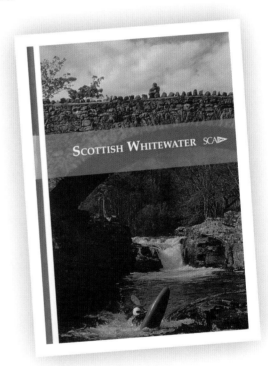

THE COVER OF THE FIRST EDITION OF THE SCOTTISH GUIDEBOOK FEATURED ANDY ON THE MORISTON.

Andy once said that he took a swim about once a year. Very few people appear to have witnessed these events. Bridget, who paddled with him all over the world for fourteen years, never saw him swim out of a boat, although she once saw him climb a vertically pinned kayak to safety! His entry for the Dall Burn in *Scottish Whitewater* is therefore remarkable on a couple of counts.

The Dall Burn

On the first and only time I have paddled the Dall Burn it was a wintry day with six inches of snow lying on the ground. Despite or perhaps because of the freezing temperatures we were keen to get on and get paddling as quickly as possible. As we flushed down the early rapids the trip was going well and we were getting in tune with the river. As we approached the first steepening I opted to run a small slab to gain an eddy which would give me a good view of the cascade below. Failing to punch the hole at the base of the slab, I had a short but frantic fight with the towback before being drawn back into the hole. A solid drilling in the hole followed. As I surfed I could feel that the situation was beginning to get out of control. Despite my best efforts I was unable to escape the clutches of the stopper and each time I rolled up I was treated to a great view of the grade 5 falls which lay immediately below and which I was now resigned to swimming over. At some point I lost my grip on the paddle and it wasn't much longer before I opted to swim. Chris Forrest, like all good paddling buddies, had by now made the bank and was watching my trashing, throwbag in hand. As I 'recirced' briefly in the hole he was able to bag me and drag my cold and shaken body to the side. The humiliation didn't stop there as, with no sign of my paddles, I had to resort to dragging my boat back down through the forest. As I staggered through the snow drifts I had plenty of time in which to contemplate my mistakes as I watched Chris run the classy stretch of water. My description of the burn is based on the memory of this cold and hazy experience so best treat it as the uncontrolled rambling of a deranged survivor. It could have been worse. At least I found my paddles in the Loch.

Every river paddler will read this with a feeling of "been there, done that", although perhaps on a lesser rapid. It's a very unusual passage to find its way into a guidebook, although not out of keeping with that guide's personal style. Most of us try to keep quiet about such experiences and few would have the self belief coupled with the lack of self importance to tell such a tale in print. It must have been an especially galling experience as Andy and Chris had walked over a mile, uphill to reach the put-in!

Mountaineers and rock climbers have been known to avoid certain climbs for years because the first ascent had been done by a notoriously hard climber. Thus Robin Smith's Thunder Rib on Sgurr a' Mhadaidh in the Black Cuillin waited a long time for a second ascent. This was partly due to Smith's awesome reputation and partly due to the brevity of his route description which recommended starting at the bottom of a prominent feature and finishing at the top. No such tendency has existed in kayaking where no record is kept of first descents but tyro paddlers might do well to look carefully at burns first paddled by Andy Jackson. A few years ago I paddled the Upper Roy with a group of central belt boaters who were still visibly shaken by their experience on the Abhainn Shlatach the previous day. One boat had been lost and others showed signs of heavy engagement. By the time they reached the harder Middle Roy they had recovered much of their self confidence and composure. Perhaps they should have taken more account of who had contributed that guide book account of the Slatach but then again, reputations can be misleading. When Thunder Rib finally received a second ascent it proved to be a fine climb but less difficult than its reputation suggested.

The appearance of the guide in 2001 did little more than confirm Jackson's status as Scotland's most prominent kayaking celebrity. Before a run down the Coe, round about 2003, he chatted amiably with some young English lads and filled them in with some details of the run when asked for information. Nobody was introduced and no names were mentioned but at the end of the river a guide-book was produced which Andy signed with the relaxed self assurance of one who can cope with fame. His reputation extended well beyond Scotland. When Eskimo paid for him to fly to the 2000 Topo Rally at Augsburg he split his free air ticket with Dave Kwant. It quickly became clear to Dave that everybody at the rally knew Jackson and before the weekend was out they had at least one more reason to remember him. There was the traditional Topo race started by Holger Machatschek, who is universally blamed for inventing the crazy little boat

ANOTHER FIRST DESCENT – ANDY PADDLES THE LOCHAY (STIRLINGSHIRE) IN 1993 THE PHOTO SHOWS ONLY PART OF THE CASCADE.

in 1980. In a Le Mans style start competitors had to run up a road, dive into the course, swim to the other side and grab their boats, which were tied together in threes! It was a race best remembered for its injuries rather than who got the champagne in the Formula One style celebrations. The Duo rodeo was pretty spectacular and then came the evening of partying. On their way back past the course Jackson suddenly began to undress and demanded that Kwant do likewise. Never one to psyche out Dave complied with minimal hesitation. As they leapt into the whitewater course Germans could be heard shouting: "You Crazy Scotsmen!", "We're doing the German thing, getting in the swing", came the reply. "You Germans like to get your kit off!" What an ambassador for Scotland! A two metre tall laddy from hell with no kilt and nothing under it either.

SKIING

Easy gully on Aonach Mòr wasn't named by skiers. It provides the easiest of winter climbing routes in and out of Coire an Lochain with only the cornice to provide any memories of steepness. For skiers it provides a challenge way beyond the run of the mill black run. For a start there is the cornice, an overhang of snow sculpted by the wind. Sometimes it is possible to slip in on the left where no cornice has formed; usually it is necessary to use a ski to hack down the overhang and create an almost vertical entry to ski across. The walls of the gully are about four metres apart which means that the skier has to be able to link short radius turns quickly and effectively or ski into the walls. Andy would ski this with ease and style. Viewed from the cornice, his back and shoulders never seemed to turn or rise and fall as he pointed straight down the gully; his legs and hips below him rhythmically working to carve one effortless turn after another. The gully opens to full corrie width 100 metres down, dropping another 260 metres to the eponymous lochan. There was an easy, efficient grace to the whole business that bordered on the beautiful, reminiscent of his paddling style. He could do this on the relatively unforgiving long narrow skis that preceded the modern fat ones that turn pigs' ears skiers into silk purses.

ANDY AT EASE OFF-PISTE, LA GRAVE, FRANCE

Andy had come to skiing as a teenager, quickly progressing to race training in Glen Shee. This was back in the '80s, that lost golden age of Scottish skiing which existed before global warming kicked in and drove average winter snow levels perhaps another 150m uphill. When he arrived in Lochaber in 1995 he had become totally focused on kayaking and abandoned snow sport. Cold dry winter days with rivers running on empty lured him back to the hill. Initially he had to be persuaded that skiing was still worthy of his time. The main problem was that he had outgrown the gear his parents had bought him at the age of fifteen. A narrow pair of giant slalom skis, 175cm long are less than ideal for somebody who is 2m tall. He really liked his boots and skied on them several times but they were size ten and his feet by then required relatively modest size twelves. A collection of borrowed gear got him through the first couple of winters in some style. At his last Fort William Mountain Film Festival he told an audience: "There is no such thing as bad weather. Only the wrong choice of toys."

Versatility is a useful attribute to those who take their pleasures in the great outdoor of Scotland and Jackson was nothing if not versatile. Dave Waugh, who had paddled with Andy since 1988 when they were teenagers, went on to become a BASI 1 ski instructor says of him: "As a skier Andy had a classic Scottish style, he was safe and strong. He had also developed very competent skills to ski any type of terrain whether it was soft bumps, chopped up crud, boiler plate ice, fresh sustrugi, wet cement, heather and grass, water, granite and even powder, which Scotland does get and you can ski if you are able to live in the vicinity and have a good work life balance, the latter being of very high importance to Andy. I loved the fact that I might get 24hrs notice that he and Bid were coming for a week's skiing holiday, whether it be when we were all getting intoxicated with Red Bull in Andorra, where we would race down through an off-piste tree section, only knowing who had survived their line when they popped out exhausted and snow covered onto a linking piste below the trees, or whether it was in France where I could show him the vastness of Les Arcs back bowls and the endless vertical meters of bumps which he loved. Although Andy did not have the same dominance of his skis as he did his kayak he was a great ambassador for this sport too. He would guide people to places on Aonach Mòr that would turn an otherwise mediocre days skiing/boarding into an epic off-piste adventure. I was proud to have joined him on such adventures and loved it when it was just him and I playing the snow stability guessing games.

Off-piste adventures often involved flying off significant cornices to land on steep slopes, not always in good visibility. This is not for the faint hearted or those who are inclined to cross their skis! Paul Currant, a snow boarder as well as a boater, has similar recollections of always pushing the limits but in a controlled manner, for example tossing snowballs onto the snow/sky-cliff edge on the back of Aonach Mòr in a whiteout to find the edge before leaping off it on skis.

Aonach Mòr, Fort William's ski area, has a world-class mountain bike downhill course and some decent ski pistes but it was what is 'over the back' that attracted Andy. A twenty minute hike from the top ski lift past Easy Gully to a variety of increasingly remote and decently steep corries and gullies, often enticing a doubtful and nervous friend along, who stumbled through the mist in the desperate hope that they would be ok because Andy would look after them. If the Braveheart Chair is working these excursions don't involve any walking or skinning once the top of the run is reached. Braveheart is rumoured to have been bought from a scrap yard in Austria and rarely functions, its mechanical unreliability being compounded by lack of snow, avalanche hazards and sundry other factors. A run over the back is generally a mission requiring a two hour budget. Jackson used to say that he began kayaking because he hated walking. He had very limited enthusiasm for ordinary hill walking but if the trip promised an adrenalin fix he would walk for miles carrying kayak or skis. When the chance arose he skied the steep, rocky, gully scarred west face of Aonach Mòr, carried his skis up the east ridge of Carn Mòr Dearg, skied down to the base of the Ben Nevis cliffs, climbed #4 Gully on the Ben and then went home via the Red Burn.

Andy carried into skiing the attitudes that characterized his kayaking. Others might be gobsmacked by what he did but he stayed within the impressive limits of his skill. He habitually wore an avalanche transceiver and carried a shovel and probe. Having spent time with Stew Rodgers making assessments for the Scottish Avalanche Information Service he knew enough about snow structures to do a Rutschblock test or to dig a pit to investigate layer bonding and snow stability.

ACCESS

Access issues followed Andy throughout his kayaking life and his contribution to the current Scottish Outdoor Access Code is part of his legacy to the Scottish outdoor community.

Various myths and misconceptions have existed on access in Scotland. Many believed that the concept of trespass did not exist in Scots law. In reality it is a civil rather that a criminal wrong. Landowners with a grievance had to take out an injunction against whoever they wished to exclude from their property. This had to be against named individuals who had already entered and declined to leave the property rather than against humanity in general. As this was a difficult and costly process it effectively meant that access to wild land in Scotland was taken as a right, often called the responsible right to roam. In the mid-nineteenth century a number of sporting estates, notably Athol Estates, sought to curtail the activities of growing numbers of town based mountaineers and hill walkers. They ran headlong into the formidable intellectual power and legal expertise of the Edinburgh middle classes and were routed in court. By the twentieth century access to the hills was rarely challenged and then generally only by non-native landowners who were ignorant of the essential difference between Scots and English law. Notable examples of this were the attempts to exclude rock climbers from Sron Ulladale in Harris in the late '60s.

By and large a similar situation existed with regard to kayaking on lowland rivers where an atmosphere of mutual respect and tolerance generally prevailed between anglers and canoeists. Very occasionally an angler from another country would challenge canoeists' presence on the river. In the early 1980s I was with a group from Kelso High School at the Edenmouth weirs on the Tweed. An irate fisherman stormed over and demanded to know if we had permission to be there. In reply to the inevitable confession that we had not he fumed: "Which school are you from? I shall tell your headmaster!" Perhaps he failed to realize that he was addressing no less a person than the son of the Duke of Roxburgh's chauffeur for, while I was still considering how to respond, the same boy leaned back in his boat and remarked: "Ah dinnae think he'll much mind. He kens fine whaur we are and whit we're daein. We cam here maist weeks." Since the days of the Reivers defence of territory has been a deeply imbedded instinct in Border Man. The tweedy gent retreated and resumed beating the waters with his rod while the kids continued to try to teach me how to do high crosses.

The relative harmony of lowland rivers was, unfortunately, less common north of the Highland line where kayaking was uncommon until the advent of plastic boats. In the late 1960s Clive Freshwater won a landmark court case against the riparian owners on the Spey who had attempted to interdict Freshwater and clients of his kayaking school. In hearings that went all the way to the House of Lords, Freshwater argued that a right of way existed on the Spey by virtue of eighteenth- and nineteenth-century log floating. A right of navigation takes precedence over all other rights and is established by forty years of uncontested use and is not lost if that use ceases. Despite this ruling kayakers continued to be harassed by gillies and water bailiffs in the Highlands. The most notorious cases were the Lyon, the Gloy, the Inverness-shire Garry and the Averon in Easter Ross. Far from being deterred, Andy was attracted to these rivers like iron filings to a magnet.

Nobody was more actively opposed to Dr Riddell's insistence that Glen Lyon was a kayak free zone. Andy Burton, a long term house sharer, distinguished from the other Andy by the sobriquet 'Mr Blobby', a burden which he has borne with great fortitude and good humour, recalls: "We were going to do the first descent of the Invervar Burn in Glen Lyon and were approached by a police officer in a Land Rover. He had had a report that our van had been seen in the glen the previous weekend when some 'no canoeing' signs had mysteriously gone missing and a tall guy with a shorter tubbier guy had been seen up a tree with a tyre lever and that we may end up in Perth Court as a report was going to the Procurator Fiscal. After we had completed a fantastic descent we were then accosted by an irate land manager on the road out of the Glen who nearly ran us off the road and shouted: "Where are my notices, I'm an educated man you know and I'll see you in court!" We found this hilarious and proceeded to go home and hide lots of signs (that we didn't have) around the house!"

An indication of how extreme the Glen Lyon situation became is that the estate put up a notice demanding that walkers do the circuit of the Glen Lyon Munros clockwise rather than anti-clockwise. It would be hard for Andy not to confront such an attitude.

Jackson was also in conflict with the Athol Estate over the use of their private road up the River Tilt up which the Estate kindly allowed hill walkers and others to drive in exchange for £5. In his youth Andy found it painful to part with money and was guilty of driving up the road without paying and encouraging others to do likewise. A number of heated exchanges did occur and the estate has ceased to allow access to vehicles. The new, liberal Scottish access code makes it clear that access does not extend to vehicles on private roads unless permission has been given. In youthful enthusiasm for boating AJ was probably guilty of pushing things a bit too far.

KENNY BIGGIN AND AJ OFF ON A PHOTOSHOOT FOR THE SCA'S ACCESS CODE LEAFLET.

We tend to mellow with age and Andy was no exception. In 2002 Andy gave up work as a Community Education Youth worker and became the Scottish Canoe Association's access officer.

Mike Dales, current SCA access officer

As the person now doing what had been Andy's final job I often feel Andy's presence, especially when I'm working on an issue that I used to chat to Andy about. Strange as it may seem, I never saw Andy in a kayak, but I did see him in a number of stuffy boring meetings. Of course, I knew how good a paddler he was and always assumed that we would paddle together some day. What those who paddled with him but never saw him in a meeting won't know, is how skilful and effective he was in those stuffy boring meetings. For someone who just wanted to be out there making films of daring descents he did have a remarkable talent to discuss issues and negotiate using diplomacy and the other interpersonal skills we all put on our CVs, but sometimes fall short on in reality.

There was one meeting I remember very clearly and Andy's ability to take every comment on its merits came across in a way that should have been recorded for a 'Dealing with difficult meetings' resource pack. The landowner representative made an outrageous comment that I immediately wanted to argue against, but the chairman gave Andy the first opportunity to respond. Andy argued the case so well that there was no need for the rest of us to say any more and the comment was retracted. The chairman moved onto the next item and the same landowner representative made the opening comment, only this time it was a very good comment that looked like having widespread acceptance. Having just put this person down Andy moved very quickly to get the first response in, and his response this time was very positive, saying; "You're absolutely right, that's exactly what we should do..." This ability to judge each issue, and each statement, on its individual merits was something that Andy was remarkably good at, and to me it was why he was proving to be such a good Access Officer.

I was working as Access Officer at the Mountaineering Council of Scotland. I was in some ways in the next nearest job to Andy's, and as a paddler myself, we spent a lot of time in 2003 and 2004 discussing the access issues of the time. The development of the Scottish Outdoor Access Code and the early days of the fight to save the River Braan from a hydro scheme seemed to be dominating Andy's time. A few years later and as a result of Andy's passing I've moved from the land to the water and taken on Andy's old job. I often look at the Code and see bits that remind me of discussions I had with Andy and I especially see the lines that Andy directly influenced. When it comes to dealing with the Braan, which is still a raging argument in the spring of 2007, I feel more than a bit angered that the energy company's unprofessional tactics, which Andy had started to rumble by late 2004, are still apparent. The fact that Andy spent his final working days fighting to save the Braan makes me determined to carry on that fight and to ensure the company gets its comeuppance. They have been prepared to sail so close to the wind in the truthfulness of some of their comments they now run the risk of being accused of perverting the course of justice.

One of Andy's great legacies was his infectious enthusiasm for canoeing. His attitude seemed to be that the water and the boat are there to be enjoyed. Access Officers often get bogged down in discussing issues and having to involve ourselves in petty arguments. Fortunately for Andy, and for the rest of us, he didn't let the word Access drag him down. He worked tirelessly for access, but in his time off he had a passion for his activity and he was an amazing bloke for encouraging others and infecting them with his great enthusiasm."

Andy's great enthusiasm was for the steep spate rivers of Scotland. Guaranteed access would be of no benefit if they were to be dammed to provide minute quantities of green energy, in a country that already generates far more electricity than it needed. Denise Marriot, one of the many to have shared Andy and Bid's home observed: "He never stopped fighting for the next river to be stolen by a hydro scheme, I remember clearly the last time we paddled the Fechlin before it was lost to one of these schemes. Those who paddled it with him on his last run there could see how hurt and angry he was at the despoiling of this wild, wonderful wee stream."

He maintained the developers had made commitments to manage the scheme in such a way as to permit kayakers some continued use of the water. This never happened and when the same promises were tried in relation to the Braan, Andy was quick to react. Clearly they had seriously underestimated their man. His friends can take some pleasure for him in the Scottish Environment Protection Agency's (SEPA) rejection of the Braan scheme.

When it was suggested that he should start a society called Kayakers for Nuclear Power he was quick to point out that the generating capacity of some major schemes such as the former BA dam at Kinlochleven and Glen Garry had actually been reduced. Carbon credit certificates are available to power companies building or renovating renewable schemes of below a specific capacity. This has led to major dams being renovated with a smaller capacity so that the carbon credit could then be sold to a major producer of greenhouse gasses. It seemed unlikely that this would significantly alter the pace of climate change. The loss of the Fechlin would not help to save the planet. It is perhaps worth noting that Andy's favourite Scottish river, the Nevis, was saved in the 1950s from a scheme to dam its magnificent gorge. Long before the word 'environment' gained any currency local people joined with admirers of the Glen from the length and breadth of Britain to oppose the loss of such magnificent scenery, thus saving the river years before anybody thought of paddling it.

At the time of writing, the Highland Council has granted planning permission for a playwave development below the tailrace of the Kinlochleven hydro-electricity scheme. Those who see the western Highlands as an area of perpetual torrential rainfall may see little need for such a project. However, anybody who has regularly paddled there will know that the rivers shrink to a trickle in summer and that the best rivers are only occasionally up and running, even in winter. An element of luck is required to be there with your gear ready when the heavens open. In the height of summer one can usually paddle the Awe, a pleasant river for early stage boaters, on a Sunday. The Morriston runs from mid-day on Tuesday to mid-day on Wednesday, giving stimulating paddling for good intermediates and better. The new access laws mean that paddlers are no longer hassled on the Garry but it still has a programme of random releases designed to make it difficult to know when its playwaves will be working. In addition to this the Spean Gorge can always be paddled and is hardest when low and the spectacular Etive is an option except during real drought. At spring tides the Falls of Lora at the mouth of Loch Etive near Oban are fun for those good enough and bold enough. To these summer options one could always add the tail race from the Fort William Aluminium works and that of the former Kinlochleven smelter.

THE AS YET UN-DEVELOPED ALCAN OUTFLOW, FORT WILLIAM.

The Kinlochleven wave just downstream of the road bridge is a permanent feature but is a bit grabby and shallow with a reputation for breaking paddles. This isn't a problem for those happy to hand surf but it is obvious that a bit of creative redesign of the river could make it much better for everybody.

Huge quantities of water, 20–45 cumecs, flow down the tail race of the Fort William smelter. Where it enters the River Lochy a wave develops either side of high tide, if river levels are right. It has to be said that it is far from being a user friendly feature but the potential to develop a world class play facility on the site is obvious in the extreme.

At the time of his death Andy had managed to get both these projects onto the drawing board and was chasing funding. The Kinlochleven project is the smaller of the two, easier to fund and build. The Fort William scheme has greater potential but also bigger problems. Built in the 1920s, the smelter takes water from Loch Laggan and Loch Treig (pronounced 'trayik') through an underground tunnel big enough to accommodate a bus, to emerge from the foothills of Ben Nevis high above the factory. In order to maximize power output the engineers tried to build the power house as low as possible. Perhaps they were a little greedy because at certain stages of the tide, water does not clear the tailrace quickly enough, starts to backfill the turbines, reduces power output and consequently profits. Alcan, the current owners of the plant, are traditionally hyper-sensitive to anything perceived as even a distant threat to their power generation. They imposed stringent conditions on the Aonach Mòr ski development in order to prevent any silting of the burns which are channelled into the system via adits. When Mr Jackson came calling with a scheme to remove water from the final section of the tail race and run it through a purpose built watersports channel they were extremely reluctant to consider the proposal at all. The plan envisaged a play wave good enough for international rodeo competitions, possibly a couple of less demanding features, a café, shop and changing rooms.

Changes in personnel at Alcan led to greater willingness to co-operate in schemes beneficial to the community and by the time of his death Andy had achieved the outline of a viable scheme for Kinlochleven and the Fort William scheme was being taken seriously and generating enthusiasm. These projects might have died with anybody else but John o'Kane, a leisure manager with the Highland Council, and Kenny Biggin were determined that this part of the Jackson legacy would not be lost. After titanic efforts the Kinlochleven wave is on the brink of being achieved and the major Fort William project is making real progress.

ABOVE, BIG WATER ON THE
HOMATHKO.
RIGHT, FROM LEFT TO RIGHT:
ANDY JACKSON, PAUL
CURRENT AND DAVE LANDIE

THE SUMMER OF '96

The expeditions which Andy undertook in the summer of '96 found him at the height of his powers. Although he would continue to run dramatic rivers it would be more and more the triumph of the mind over an increasingly troublesome body.

The first trip with Dave Landie and Paul Currant was to British Columbia. The Homathko had been first run in 1987 and they were aiming for what was believed to be the 4th descent. This article by Andy was published posthumously, nine years later in *Canoe & Kayak UK*.

Trial by nature: Hairy times on the Homathko

"How's that spot look?" I asked. "There's some sand to doss on but it's awful close to the edge of the forest." Paul shouted back as he peered nervously into the undergrowth. "Well, it'll have to do, or we'll be boating in the dark." "Hello, are there any bears in there?" shouted Paul as he gingerly approached our chosen campsite. Grinning broadly at the silent reply we climb out of our boats trying not to look quite so scared as we feel.

"That's the great thing about this trip," trumps up Dave, "you never know which will kill you, the bears or the river. It kind of keeps you guessing."

Suddenly Paul came rushing back towards us, shouting a garbled warning. In the ensuing panic, Dave and I dive for the same kayak in a desperate attempt to get back afloat. Not daring to take a second glance, I could only imagine the scene of carnage behind me, as the charging grizzly ripped my friend apart. Our panicked bid for escape ended as it dawned on us that the only sound of bodily damage was Paul splitting his sides as he enjoyed our Laurel and Hardy antics. "Only joking," Paul grinned. "That is so unfunny," came the less than chuffed reply; but at least the tension of the moment was relieved. "Oh God, it's only day one and we are already a bag of nerves," but it was already too late for thoughts like that. We were more than committed now.

ABOVE, GLACIER VIEWED ON THE FLIGHT IN (RIGHT).

We were three Scottish kayakers feeling well out of our depth. The River Homathko has carved a direct path from the interior of British Columbia to the Pacific Ocean. Foregoing the 600km detour of its more mature neighbour, the Fraser River, the Homathko cuts through the Coastal Mountain Range in a series of deep and remote gorges.

Our journey began at Tatllayoko Lake, a dramatic spot where the seemingly endless interior plateau meets a chain of unbroken 3,000 metre peaks. The scenery was breathtaking and not just a little intimidating. We knew that once we left the calm waters of the lake we would be on our own; no roads, paths or people soften the wilderness in the Homathko Valley. On the eve of our departure a kind family who owned a ranch at the edge of the mountains befriended us. Their family had first settled in this area more than a century ago and they were the original pioneers. As we enjoyed the warmth of a roaring log fire and their companionship they regaled us with tales of the, often hard, life on an isolated ranch. As the evening rolled on our fear of all things bear shaped intensified with each new story of death at the hands of the grizzly monsters. The family described the Homathko Valley as impenetrable on foot and they described the river viewed from the air as funnelling through enormous cataracts blocked by house-sized boulders. They assured us we would never make it and asked if we wouldn't rather try an easier river elsewhere! We in turn reassured them that we knew what we were doing and that the river had already been paddled some years ago. The morning saw us packing in an excited mood. Our newfound friends waved us good-bye. They were sure that we would never be seen again, and looked at us pityingly as we promised to radio them once we had finished the river.

Once afloat, five days of food and cold weather camping gear gave the boats an uneasy heavy feeling. Nevertheless, we were glad to be off and paddled the few kilometres along the lake to the river mouth at a pace just short of a sprint, eager to catch our first glimpse of the Homathko. As with any long trip we expected that the river would start fairly small and that the volume would increase as tributaries added to the flow. Our river notes from a previous group also indicated that the first day's paddling was quite straightforward, grade 3.

As we paddled the first few kilometres we revelled in our situation. Snowy peaks began to surround us. On either side hanging glaciers dropped almost to the river; the scale of the place was incredible. A large tributary joined from the left and the water took on a new and more powerful feel. The first big rapids gave us a taste of unknown difficulties to come. The cold grey glacier melt warned us that mistakes would be heavily punished.

ABOVE, CREEKING AROUND WHISTLER WHILST WAITING FOR THE LEVEL TO DROP ON THE HOMATHKO

Peeking from my bivi bag I watched as the shadows of the night retreated into the forest and I struggled from the warmth of my pit to get a fire going and breakfast under way. Over porridge we discussed the river ahead of us and searched the map playing the 'name that glacier' game. After agreeing a truce, which prohibited any more jokes about bears, we could delay no longer and squeezed all the gear back into the kayaks and took to the water. The morning was cold and we were immediately into big rapids. We passed some great playholes and surf waves without giving them a second glance, nobody wanted to take any unnecessary risks, this was no place to fool around. Hours spent freestyling and creeking in the past seemed like a cheap thrill from another life, all that mattered now was getting downstream and not swimming. To take a swim on a river like this was our collective idea of a worst nightmare. To lose a kayak complete with gear would spell disaster. The unhappy swimmer on reaching the 'safety' of the bank would quickly become separated from those chasing his kayak and would be left to face bears, glaciers and hunger alone and all in his wetsuit boots! The speed of the river and the harsh terrain on the bank only served to exaggerate the problem, a few kilometres could be travelled by kayak in an hour or two but might take several days of hapless struggle on the bank.

The water was good, our boat scouting skills were being pushed, but as the gorge walls closed in we knew that we had arrived at what the map ominously referred to as the Great Canyon of the Homathko. A steepening of the river forced a lengthy bank scout. After much 'umming' and 'ahhing' about the crucial hole we decided to portage the first half of the rapid. Even so the last 200 meters of the grade 5+ rapid blew us away and we all had a small personal epic to recount upon regrouping above the next steep volumous section. Again we portaged, critically aware of our situation and the need to keep moving downstream. It would be a shame to have to stretch five days food to last two weeks! Back on the water we had barely gone half a kilometre before progress was again halted. Before us the river dropped in a long unbroken cataract haunted by logjams and huge pourovers. Paddling the rapid was out of the question, but what of the portage? On either bank great slabs of granite dropped sheer to the river. A desperate chicken shoot would allow us to run the top quarter of the rapid and commit us to finding a way round on river right. As the cliffs on river left looked equally unfeasible we decided to give the right side a go. The chicken shoot behind us, we drew on our collective lack of rock climbing experience and tackled the cliffs. An hour or so of futile effort later and we began to feel just a little bit trapped. Perhaps we could boat the rapid after all, "that hole doesn't look so bad from here." But it did, and we were forced to retreat. A

DAVE AND ANDY DEEP IN ONE OF THE
HOMATHKO'S GORGES.

ACTION ON THE
HOMATHKO RIVER.

combination of climbing and swimming back upstream across eddies brought us once again to the top of the carnage. One scary ferry glide later and we began to explore the cliffs on river left. The words of those at the ranch echoed mockingly in my head as I began to doubt our information on the river and the feasibility of our trip. Perched on a small ledge mid portage we stopped for our fix of power bars and trail mix. Dave as ever tried to look on the bright side. "Well at least we haven't seen any bears." Paul and I considered throwing him into the river, but in the end, sacrificing Dave to the river gods proved unnecessary. They choose to smile on us of their own accord, offering a slimy crack system by which we could bypass both the cliffs and rapid. Back in our boats, on the happy side of the Great Canyon, our spirits rose and we were treated to some great whitewater. With confidence growing, we relished each big rapid and admired the incredible scenery. The arrival of Doran Creek, tumbling into the river over a waterfall on the left and an imposing gateway of granite cliffs warned of a new chapter in the river. Picking a spot in the forest we collapsed and built a fire, noticeably less worried about the bears after a ten-hour river day.

The trick with multi-day boating is to try and get as much food as possible from your boat eaten at the start of the trip, that way you'll have less to carry. Unfortunately all in our party were wise to this scam and the ensuing argument at each mealtime was inevitable: "No really I insist let's eat some of my pasta and tuna."

The next day began with yet more portaging. Dragging a loaded boat in the forest is simply not a nice activity. Do you keep your dry suit on and get soaked with sweat or do you take it off and let the mosquitoes eat you. I chose the worst option, which is to get soaked with sweat and then when you can stand the heat no more, take your dry suit off and let the mozzies harass you as well! Three torturous hours later we regained the river by lowering the boats down a steep gully into a serious looking gorge. We shared the eddy at the base of the rope lower with huge pieces of driftwood. The rock scenery was incredible. We felt dwarfed by it all. Crashing waves and surging boils conspired to keep us on the edge of our seats, minds focused as we tuned in to the river. Nothing mattered but the water ahead. As we exited the gorge, high as kites, Mount Waddington and the Tiedemann Glacier filled the skyline. We are carried ever westwards.

LONG RAPIDS LEFT LITTLE TIME TO ADMIRE SCENERY.

From our river notes we guessed that the rapid before us was called 'The Bet' and a monster it was too. The river flowing from the Tiedemann glacier had virtually doubled the volume of the Homathko, which was now a conveyer belt of cold water moving at an alarming speed. The appearance of 'The Bet' had us scampering for the bank. Here the river accelerated as it became funnelled by bedrock intrusions. The only feasible line meant working to stay left at the entrance, slamming through a series of meaty hydraulics and somehow managing to stay upright and above the water in order to make a crucial move right away from the jaws of the last stopper. We stared into the depths of the bottom hole, mesmerised. What would happen to you if you went in there? This rapid was well named, the whole thing was a bit of a gamble; there was no way to protect the bottom hole and no room for error. I could feel the excitement mounting within me. Questions and nagging doubts had to be put aside. Only when I could visualise the rapid being run successfully would I be ready to paddle. Paul provided that vision in a very real way. I watched through the back of a camera lens as he made his run. As soon as he was in the rapid the enormity of the thing hit me. I hate to think what was going through Paul's mind. At any one time only a small part of him or his boat was visible above the water, it seemed that he would just be swallowed whole. His line was good; he made a vital couple of strokes to avoid the final hole. Dave and I took our turn, and as we finished the rapid we knew that this was what we came for. All well and good, as long as the worst of it was now behind us!

Throughout the trip we had been relying on a period of cold and unsettled weather to keep the river at a reasonable level. If the air temperature began to rise the glaciers feeding the river would melt faster and the water level would rise dramatically, not what we needed. By the evening of the fourth day I would have settled for a little less rain and a little more heat. Collecting driftwood, we built an extravagantly large fire for warmth and as a bear deterrent. Gathered round the blaze we slept uneasily, losing the fight to stay dry.

Next morning climbing out of wet sleeping bags into wet paddling gear we decided to go for broke and try and finish the trip that day rather than face another wet and cold bivouac. Our destination was the Scar Creek logging camp where we hoped to charter a plane to fly us back over the mountains to the put-in. We knew that there was also a good chance of scrounging a warm bed and food at a logging camp and with this in mind we packed the boats quickly and hurried off downstream. The day passed as a blur, the river careering wildly between huge granite walls. We were covering ground really fast and at every blind corner my mind went into overdrive, I was appalled at the thought of being swept into another grade 6 section of certain doom! Huge rapids came and went but all were 'a go'. True to character the Homathko kept us guessing to the bitter end. As we were flushed from the last canyon down a huge wave train Dave attempted to snatch defeat from the jaws of victory and dropped into a monster hole. A short but ferocious trashing was enough to rattle his marbles but not to unseat him from his Diablo. With the slightly sad feeling of a fairground ride slowing down we drifted with the now lazy river and took in the scenery as granite cliffs gave way to river delta. Our trial by nature was over and the verdict was that the Homathko had delivered all that we could have hoped for.

In 2007 Paul Currant, no shrinking violet, confirmed that the big fall that was so hard to portage has now been paddled at a lower flow. He considered it unthinkable at the level at which he encountered it. It was of Andy's insistence that they should scout ahead at this point that Paul said, "Sometimes it seemed as though he had an extra sense of the river and its dangers."

TURKISH DELIGHT

Andy tended to revisit favoured paddling venues. He went to Nepal no less than five times. Norway, another favourite, endured no less than six trips, four of them consecutively in 1999, 2000, 2001 and 2002. He went to Turkey twice; the first time in 1996. He returned with Bridget, Paul Currant and Dave Waugh for a second slice in 1999. This article, written by Andy and printed in *Canoeist* magazine in 1997, relates his experience on that first trip.

Problem Yok!

As the arriving bus pulled to a halt outside the small roadside café my heart sank. The luxury coach, as it declared itself to be was, indeed, surprisingly modern for this part of the world but it was unfortunately rather full and even worse, there was no way on earth that smelly river runners complete with kayaks and gear could possibly be accommodated and our long wait at the side of the road looked set to continue.

I don't know if it was the prospect of tourist money or just the usual friendship and willingness to help that we experienced throughout our trip but the driver leapt from his cab with a huge smile on his face. After the usual greetings and much shaking of hands the driver, still grinning widely, gestured that we should climb aboard. With our flicked-through-the-phrasebook-on-the-plane grasp of Turkish we pointed at our boats and gear and tried to explain where we wanted to go. Talking at us at machine gun speed and feverishly nodding his head, the driver again gestured that we should get on the bus. Obviously we had a communication problem and tried again to explain that there was nowhere to put the boats. "Problem yok, problem yok," the driver nodded, grabbing the nearest boat and dragging it towards the bus.

"What do you mean no problem; you don't have a roof rack, mate," Howie added helpfully, but the grinning driver was not to be deterred. Still looking at each other a little bemused, we helped pass the kayaks up onto the roof of the coach and, with a mixture of disbelief and concern, watched as some string appeared and the boats were hastily tied to a plastic skylight. With the boats on the roof (secured would be the wrong word) we squeezed into the coach and found ourselves a seat.

"Problem yok," the driver again assured us as we set off up the road at breakneck pace and we smiled at each other nervously and tried hard not to think of our three Diablos complete with the skylight vanishing over the cliffs which lay at the side of the mountain road.

HIGH FLOWS ON THE ÇORUH.

We had just finished the River Çoruh, an absolute gem of a river tucked away in north-eastern Turkey, ten days of grade 3 and 4 whitewater with one enormous grade 5 thrown in for good measure. At this high water time of year the river has a lovely continuous nature. In its entire length there is barely a pool and certainly no flat sections. The Çoruh, on its journey from the mountains to the Black Sea, has carved a passage through several deep and dramatic gorges, creating exciting and constantly changing river scenery. For us the journey was like an elongated beach holiday, every evening whiled away on a different riverside campsite while every day brought new rapids and dream surf waves.

The start of our journey on this incredible river had been almost overwhelming. Putting on in the heat of a steamy Turkish afternoon it seemed as though the entire town of Ispir had come to see us depart. I looked at the initial set of rapids running past the edge of this ancient town clustered around the teetering ruins of a fairytale castle; they looked fast and powerful. Almost melting inside my paddle jacket and very aware of the weight of gear in my heavily laden boat, I took to the water. Immediately the current had me. Tired arms fought to gain the centre of the river, my body suddenly weak from the trials of several days' travelling and the exertion of carrying the boats to the put-in. As my small boat sped into the first rapid the local crowd cheered and excited children chased me down the riverbank. A massive cushion of water filled my vision and, hanging in there, I made it through the first corner. Pulsing waves flushed me away from the town and crowds and I had soon joined Ant,

Ant's architectural creations, which normally took several hours to erect and always ended up resembling something from a Mad Max movie. Come the morning we would eventually stir after several cups of coffee and begin the process of packing all that gear back in the boats. Ideally, this would include a good game of who could find the biggest spider, frog, snake, etc and hide it in his friend's kayak without him noticing. All too soon it would be time to get back on the water and surf, surf, surf.

On our fifth day on the river we arrived at Yusufeli, a chance to resupply and enjoy cold beers. By now the river had grown in volume still further and as we dragged ourselves away from the comforts of this small town we knew that the best rapids were still to come.

House Rock is, perhaps, not the most imaginative name for the biggest rapid on the river but it is descriptive. Crashing through a river-wide entry hole, the enormous volume of water is then forced in a maelstrom of fold-ing waves between the undercut cliffs on river right and the colossal boulder, which occupies the centre of the river. The paddler must get through the hole, avoid being splatted on House Rock and retain sufficient con-trol to avoid the final nasty pourovers on the outside of the corner. It's a long lonely rapid. Scrambling up a scree slope, we enjoyed the luxury of scouting the rapid from the road high above the river and it was with a pleasant detached feeling that we viewed the carnage below. Pulling the camera excuse, I lingered on awhile as I watched Howie and Ant descend the scree slope and prepare to make their runs. I watched as airbags

spluttering excitedly in the first eddy. "It's really fast, eh?" Ant enthused and I had to agree. Settling into the rhythm of the river, it was an enormous relief to cool off in the rushing waters and we soon had our heavily laden beasts under control. As a great river experience unfolded before us it was three happy kayakers who sat round that first campfire.

As the days rolled by we settled into a routine. Each afternoon around three o' clock, when we felt it was time to stop boating and resume lying around in the sun, we would look for a spot to make camp. Typically, Ant would create a bivouac for the three of us, using the handy flysheets which we had brought for this task, while Howie and I would get a fire going and kick back with cups of tea. This gave us plenty of time to mock

LEFT, CREEKING ON THE BARHAL. ABOVE, HITCHING A LIFT.

were inflated, boats sponged out, equipment stowed, buoyancy aids adjusted, footrests checked, sunblock applied, toggles twiggled and eventually it was Ant who broke and reluctantly climbed into his boat to go first. Getting the first half of the rapid real sweet, he appeared dwarfed by the exploding mass of water around him. He was flipped. I didn't know where and I scanned the rapid with my camera, soon spotting his upturned boat just past House Rock. Eventually he pulled himself together and rolled up way over on river right. Dragged along the wall, he didn't stand a chance and he disappeared into the worst of the pourovers. For a while I saw nothing then I spotted him a long way downstream, a little shaken up and swimming but otherwise okay. Signalling to Howie that Ant was out of his boat, I wondered what to do next. I started to leg it down the road after Ant, then realized I didn't have a throwline. I ran back upstream, wondering what I was going to do on a river this big

with only 15m of rope. I spotted Howie running round in circles at river level – a truck came by. I tried to flag it down but it was going the wrong way. Howie resigned himself to paddling the rapid in a chase boating role and I ran back down the road just for show. Meanwhile, half a mile or so downstream Ant had done the heroic thing and swum his boat, paddle and battered body to the bank. As I walked back upstream I watched Howie survive the rapid. He celebrated his successful descent with a scream of delight and I realized that I was fresh out of excuses. Two truck drivers had stopped at the top of the road. One of them waved at the rapid below and then at me, shrugging his shoulders in a questioning manner. I pointed to my kayak waiting for me at the start of the rapid and give him a thumbs up. Looking suddenly worried, he drew his finger across his throat, shook his head and let out a long slow whistle. "Problem yok," I told him … and hoped I meant it.

ABOVE, PADDLING WITH ICEBERGS.
LEFT, PAUL CURRANT (LEFT) AND ANDY JACKSON
BELOW THE THIEVES' WATERFALL, ICELAND.

ICELAND

In 1997 Shaun Baker was approached by a programme researcher on behalf of Transworld Sports. They were pursuing an unhealthy interest in what they called extreme sports. Shaun had just set the world record for paddling the highest water fall yet survived. They wanted to film him in action on Iceland on some big unpaddled drops. Baker was interested but said he'd need time to put together a backup team of safety kayakers. Before very long the researcher was back announcing that he had recruited Paul Currant and Andy Jackson as safety cover. Shaun had paddled with both on the rodeo circuit, knew and liked them but his ideas on backup went way beyond a couple of other high end paddlers. He liked to have a few climbers, rope access and rescue specialists on hand. The only trouble with top class safety boaters was they would want to run the stuff as well, unlikely to be content to simply offer cover at the bottom of drops. Against his better judgment, Shaun agreed to go ahead. Here is Andy's account of what followed, originally printed in *Playboating*.

The 'High 5' whiter than white challenge – Guaranteed or your money back

"You're going to call the program what?" I started to question the sanity of our director, Steve, and wondered if perhaps we had been a little too hasty in adopting our role as TV stars. I'd known from the start that a free trip would have its down side (like having to look a complete prat in front of my friends and family). Was the price now starting to look a little high? Well, was a bit late for such thoughts. We had sold our souls and now it was time to swallow our pride.

Sideways glances were exchanged between Paul, Shaun and I as Steve enthused about the script. Apparently some Viking cartoon character called 'Bodo' had set us the ridiculously named challenge. We were to travel to Iceland with a tick list of tasks, in an attempt to satisfy his Nordic appetite for disaster (and presumably enhance the 'prat' factor). In the space of a week Bodo required us to find and make the first descent of a river, paddle a previously un-run waterfall, surf on a volcanic black sand beach and kayak through extremes of temperatures, amongst icebergs and hot springs. Having resigned our-selves to our fate, we sat down to film the first of many interviews. Paul and I thought it best to let Shaun lead the way and show us what this TV thing was all about. He is after all an official movie star! One by one we took our turn and were soon all enthusing about our challenge, cursing Viking Bodo, but beginning to thoroughly over play the part. Oh well, at least we were here.

And what a place it is. Iceland is an island of contrasts, beautiful yet barren. Glaciers pour from mist shrouded hills through what can only be described as a moon-scape. The warmth and hospitality of the Icelanders serves only to emphasize the unforgiving nature of the land. Wasting no time, we got to work on our slightly surreal task. Our job would be made easier by two factors. Firstly, there is no shortage of whitewater in Iceland. Swollen rivers descend every valley, fed by mostly unseen ice caps, the unique geology ensuring that waterfalls and canyons abound. Secondly, the film crew had borrowed a rather amazing 4x4 truck for our transport. The 'Hummer' came complete with a driver/guide, GPS, radios and a host of other gizmos. We would certainly have no problem getting around.

Settling into the kayaking, we set off to show the camera crew what us river-runner-types were all about. The locals pointed us in the direction of a creek, which we were told would be a first descent. A quick scout revealed a series of un-runnable falls followed by some nice grade 5, including a 9 metre drop. Steve assured us that in the make believe world of TV the lower section of river would suffice and we were soon enjoying the

run-in to the fall. It was raining heavily and the glacier melt water was freezing cold, so by the time we arrived at the drop we were all rather chilly. Isn't it funny how drops which look okay when viewed from above, take on a new menace as you peer at them from water level. We obviously hadn't learned this lesson as Paul, Shaun and I came face to face with the stark realisation that we didn't want to run the drop. The camera crew took our decision surprisingly well considering they were soaked to the skin, mildly hypothermic and had very little foot-age to show for our day's effort.

We retreated to the warmth of the hotel, where our hosts confounded our problems by serving up the Icelandic national dish of sheep's head and rotting shark. Shaun did himself proud as Mr Extreme, plucking out and swal-lowing a sheep's eye whole. I got the sneaking feeling that it was Bodo 1 – Kayakers 0. We would have to pull out all the stops tomorrow or the film crew would begin to wonder if we were worth the air fares.

The next day the sun shone and we were soon whoop-ing and hollering as we saw our next river. The 'Thieves Waterfall' is so named because it's a place where, in times gone by, robbers and the like were thrown into the falls as punishment. History doesn't record how many, if any, of the unfortunate souls survived but looking at the size of the stopper it's easy to understand that this would be an effective punishment. Steve briefed us on the script and told us this would be our final challenge, a chance to prove ourselves and cleanse our souls of any previous wrong doing. Having set up the cameras and got the inevitable interviews out of the way, we got on with the paddling. The drop was a real cracker. A big volume fall over a wide shelf, 10 metres high. In the centre of the river huge boils and spray demonstrated the power of what must be a terminal hole. We chose a route near the right hand bank with a good straight run in and a powerful, but flushing, hole to land in. We ran the fall several times each, the camera crew lapping up every minute of it and capturing all the angles. And it wasn't long before we were calling each other 'dude' and indulging in High 5 celebrations in the eddy.

Paul spotted another line in the middle of the river and we opted to give it a go. This final run of the fall involved beaching on a rocky island in the centre of the river, on the lip of the drop. From this airy vantage point we were treated to a close up view of the worst of the hole. Paul led the way, with a route, which clipped the worst of the hole, but a flattish landing saw him safely through. Shaun took on slightly more of the hole and disappeared into the maw below. There was nothing to be seen of him for what seemed like an eternity. Suddenly his empty Topo could be seen being churned around at the base of the fall. With a rising sense of panic I searched anxiously for any sign of Shaun. It seemed incredible yet inevitable that our antics could have gone this wrong. I stood impotently on the lip of the fall and wondered what previous crime Shaun was being punished for. Eventually he surfaced, a staggering 20 metres downstream of the fall, just breathing and no more. He was helped to the bank by Paul where he made a spluttering recovery. I was still perched on the small island and, having just witnessed Shaun's experience, was keen not to repeat it. As I weighed

ANDY RUNS THE THEIVES' WATERFALL ONCE AGAIN FOR THE CAMERAS.

TERNS IN A SURREAL LANDSCAPE.

was spiced up by the thought of what would happen if one of these monsters flipped over. As we nosed our way through the maze of ice, a few large splashes accompanied by the noise of tons of falling ice served to remind us of the danger. Possibly the most exciting flat paddle I've ever experienced.

As the week wore on, we had all but completed our challenge. Finally we were getting the better of Viking Bodo, but time was running out. Our journey had led us to a river on the far side of Iceland, a long way from our homeward flight. As we finished the river we weighed up our situation. It was a good eight hours of cross-country driving to Reykjavik and our flight was at seven the next morning. A mad dash ensued as we packed our gear and got started on our all-night drive. But the film crew must have been in league with Bodo, as they insisted that we take time for one last interview before beginning our drive. You know the kind of thing. "Why do we go boating" and, "Isn't it cold and scary?" Thrusting a microphone towards Paul, the director asked in his most dramatic voice, "So Paul, when you paddle all these really dangerous rivers, do you get the feeling that a 'greater being' is controlling your destiny? Do you believe in river gods?", "Ahh, nunmhh, no, not really" came Paul's cringed reply.

up my options I realised that a helicopter rescue was probably beyond the budget of the film crew and I knew I had no choice but to run the drop. I chose the highest point of the drop and went for the forty foot boof move. In my highly motivated state I was prepared to ignore the inevitable spinal injury of a pancake landing. In fact I was prepared to face anything rather than going into the hole. My fight had a predictably sore end but I was able to paddle clear of the base of the fall. The film crew loved the drama of it all and indulged Shaun in a particularly long and painful interview about how it feels to come so close.

Back on the road again we tracked down some icebergs and enjoyed a paddle in an incredibly scenic situation. Exploring ice caves and seal launching down icebergs

"How about you say you're actually deeply superstitious or something like that", prompted Steve.

"Oh okay, whatever." Paul looked to Shaun and me for support and found none. The interview began again. "So Paul, do you ever find yourself affected by superstition when you're paddling?" Paul's reply: "Ah, yes. I often wonder if perhaps a greater power is controlling things, river gods or something. You get the picture! "

Eventually we got underway and raced for the airport. Not to be beaten by Bodo, we stopped for one last paddle at 4 am in a hot spring, and completed the last stage of our challenge. The back drop of a thermal power station made for a bizarre scene as we launched into the steaming, naturally heated water in the middle of the night. A strange end to a strange trip. But hey don't take my word for it. You can see for yourself on Transworld Sports.

This was the first and probably only descent of the Waterfall of Thieves. There is a dam upstream which normally reduces the flow to a trickle but by chance the turbines were being repaired. The fall had been restored to its awesome glory.

Paul Currant still has vivid recollections of the event.

"I don't know how big the fall is … it's height gets shrunk a bit due to the width of the thing … it's more the volume of water and the overall power of the thing which is the issue … but we all agreed this drop was dangerously big for boofing with a risk of spinal injury/compression. Shaun had developed a technique of forcing his toes forward to make the boat dive nose first hence avoiding getting your spine compressed when the boat lands too flat off a big fall. Neither Andy or I had this move wired … I lobbed off first and thought ouch my boat's too flat but with this angle it skimmed nicely out away from the hole at the bottom. I waited in the eddy someway downstream of the thundering drop. Shaun came next having checked the line with Andy stationed on his little rock. He made his diving move but the boat slightly over-rotated into the fall and ended up behind it … He was gone for ages. I paddled back up into the boiling water towards the fall scanning the surface for any sign of him. Then when I thought he couldn't survive any more time under water he came up purple, gasping and delirious. I got him and his kit over to the bank and thanked the Lord that he was still with us. From our rescue point further downstream we could just see Andy's head and some desperate signalling ensued. Andy had no option but to paddle the drop since there was no way back upstream from his tiny rock perched in the middle of this huge river on the edge of the fall. We somehow communicated and decided that the best option was for him to paddle a slightly higher but less powerful part of the fall, river left of mine and Shaun's line. This he did and made sure his boat was flying well out from the hole."

In a subsequent radio interview Shuan Baker explained the camera crew couldn't see, or film Paul's line after he left the top of the fall. Keen to give the television company value for money Shaun ran a line they could see. He went deep but briefly re-surfaced behind the fall which hit him with massive force ripping away his paddle and thrust him back down deep again. Very deep, and since he didn't sense any likelihood of his surfacing quickly he kicked off his boat. Losing his most buoyant asset he shot down, deeper and deeper into the green room and beyond into utter blackness. For those who have wondered what drowning is like, he recalls excruciating pain in every part of his body. Finally the undertow dragged him along the riverbed until he could soar, like superman, to the surface to be rescued by a more than slightly relieved Paul Current. Shaun was so tired and out of breath that he had to make a conscious effort to breath, a situation he compared to being born. Currant, an anaesthetist, comforted him with the observation that he often saw corpses with healthier colour.

At the top of the fall Andy was in an unenviable situation. He had begun to have a series of injuries and health problems that would plague the last eight years of his life, including a back injury sustained while skiing that made his decent of the Thieves Fall even more traumatic than it might have been. Shaun remembers him pacing up and down the rock that ran back 8m from the edge of the fall, getting into his boat and getting out again to re-check the line. And then he hit it, centimetre perfect and the biggest boof that Shaun had ever seen, way out from the bottom of the fall followed. A very sore back was his reward. Not the boy for the seriously hard stuff? Everything, as they say, is relative.

MAKING THE MOVES AND THE MOVIES

The Iceland challenge was far from the only video material that featured Andy Jackson. He was a film maker of some talent himself and collaborated with others, notably Steve Rogers, Dave Kwant and Andy Watt in producing a number of features that were well worth watching. *Lochaber Lifestyles*, in which he and Callum Anderson worked with Steve Rogers, won the top award at the Edinburgh Mountain Film Festival. A blend of dramatic action and wry humour it was, needless to say, very well received at the Fort William Festival. The Nevis, up and roaring, was Andy's favourite Scottish river, possibly his favourite river anywhere, so *Lifestyles* was definitely a labour of love. It was filmed on several trips to the river. Towards the end, as the Fort William Mountain Film Festival loomed, it was a race against time with the outcome depending on whether Andy and Steve 'Sick Boy' Rogers could get enough good health days and synchronize them. Helmet cameras, bow and bank cameras brought the viewer right into the action. It ends with a series of horrific trashings endured in a variety of intimidating ditches and a grateful acknowledgment to the Belford Hospital, a joke that was especially well received at a time when health service bureaucrats were keen to close the busiest mountain trauma hospital in Europe outside Chamonix. It has to be said that no dumb animals were harmed in the making of that movie. *Lifestyles* was his ultimate achievement in a video making habit that had been developing for some time.

On his first trip to Nepal with Chris Dickinson, Andy and Chris carried a Super-8 cine camera, the footage from which was later edited by Chris to make a record of the trip.

Long before he got into video Andy was interested in creating good stills images of boating. He rejected waterproof compact film camera in favour of a Nikon SLR in a waterproof case. Photographs had to be taken from the bank but this gave a good steady platform for the camera and often better vantage points. As video cameras shrunk it became possible to fit them into boats. *Another Kogg Day* was a precursor to *Lochaber Lifestyles*, filmed by Dave Kwant it featured the usual mix of rain soaked landscapes, spate burns, dripping highland cattle, parties, optimism and dramatic boating action.

The '99 trip to Norway, with Dave Waugh and Mark Sherif, saw him paddling again with German legend and film maker Olaf Obsommer. Both produced a video called *The Sick Line*. Obsommer's effort was probably the more sophisticated, as one might expect from a professional film maker. It also focused more on personalities, something from which Andy's natural modesty, perhaps a product of Scottish reticence, would make him shy away. Both video's featured dramatic paddling on big uncompromising rivers combined with the inevitable electric guitar background. It lacked the cameo interviews, voice overs and humour that made *Lochaber Lifestyles*. Nevertheless the camera work was as technically impressive as the boating was dramatic. The later videos, made with Steve Rogers clearly benefited from the collaborative approach that wasn't available in the Norway film.

Jackson could, of course, perform in front of the camera as well. He was keen to take Dave Kwant to Nepal to film the 2001 paragliding and kayaking trip. Andy Watt treasures footage of Jackson ripping up The Falls of Lora in full flood.

In October 2003, fourteen months before his death Andy made a video of a 220 mile journey through the Grand Canyon of the Colorado, in which he displayed equal skill as a paddler and camera man. This expedition, accompanied by American legend Whit Deschner, was to be Jacko's last big trip. His energy levels depleted, he spent long spells relaxing on a raft, until the whitewater sections materialized then he struggled into his kayak and did his thing in a manner that 99.9% of totally hale and healthy boaters would envy. He proved to be a wonderfully laid back, relaxed, wry front man for his video masterpiece.

Had he survived it is more than just possible that Andy would have sought his next frontier in the field of adventure sport film production. His premature death must have deprived us of a great deal of good entertainment.

JACKSON ON THE COLORADO IN 2003

RIGHT, STUNNING SCENERY
AND CONTINUOUS WATER ON
THE RIO MAIPO.
BELOW, ANDY BOATS 'THE
SEVEN TEACUPS' SECTION ON
THE RIO CLARO. ANDY SAW A
SIMILAR PHOTO AS A CHILD,
WHICH INSPIRED HIM TO
PERSIST WITH KAYAKING AND
VISIT CHILE SOME DAY.

CHILE

Antarctica and Africa seem to be the only continents that didn't receive a state visit from Andy Jackson. Bridget has been skiing in Africa and done a bit more there besides so that leaves Antarctica alone for her to visit. Here then is the story of their first visit to South America (joined by Dave Landie and Iain McKendry) written by Bridget and printed in *Playboating* magazine.

Rio Claro

Our ancient guidebook mentioned an upper stretch of the Rio Claro, the 'Veintedos' section or 22 falls. The advice given was that these had been run with 2–4 cumecs of water (a trickle). More water and the river would become impossible to paddle and, with its completely smooth water washed basalt walls, equally impossible to portage or climb out of.

An afternoon spent dicing with death and getting ever hotter, dustier, more thirsty and scratched as we peered into the clear water of the stunningly inviting gorge way below, was enough to convince us that we really wanted to do this run. We hadn't seen any definite portages – just lots of fun drops and one or two that looked kinda tricky – and that was from 200 feet up.

That evening we endlessly discussed the day ahead, and I for one spent the night tossing and turning as glimpses of the river floated through my mind. Had we really managed to see all the drops from the overhanging cliff edge? Was there too much water? Did I really want to run that big fall? How big was it anyway? What about that drop we couldn't quite see, and that river-wide ledge near the end? One thing was certain – once we were in, there was no way out except by boat. This was going to be one of the most committing runs of my life. Was I really ready for it?

Next morning, having chatted up the National Park's head Ranger and gained access to the washed out four wheel drive track that led to the put-in, we rallied our misused pickup through the bush. This process elicited manic grins from Andy and Dave, who took turns in the driver's seat and gasps of terror from those not behind the wheel. A couple of miles later, we surveyed the scratched vehicle and the huge boulders in the track ahead, and admitted that it was time to walk.

Soon we were deep in the gorge, looking around us at a world of brilliant sunlight, sparkling water and deep shadows, the only noise the tumbling of water and the almost audible throb of our hearts. The moment of truth had arrived. A major horizon line in front of us, a knot of fear in my stomach. Andy cheerfully scrabbled out on the lip of the fall with his video camera and gave us the thumbs up. Iain was first and then it was my shot. A clean fall, a little over 30 feet. I didn't want to land flat – too many of my friends had hurt themselves that way, but I didn't want to pencil in. Seconds later, I surfaced in the sunshine at the base of the fall, a huge grin, relief, elation, time to relax and watch the others.

Then round the corner to the next horizon line and the next psyche-up. As drop after drop went smoothly, I started to relax and feel less trapped. The river felt so benign, so friendly, and the gorge walls, although completely un-climbable, felt less threatening. And then I realised that we were fast approaching the partially hidden drop that had left me tossing and turning in my sleep the previous night.

From our eddy, the water swirled down a narrow channel over a small drop and then disappeared. Beside us, the cliffs rose in a sheer wall of rock. There was no way to get out, no way to scout, or was there? Attached to a throw line, Andy swam off down the pool to a rock shelf and scrambled out. Dave followed, and the two of them inched along the ledge to the corner and a view. They signalled it was okay and Dave came back to explain the line. I was third to run, but somehow after dreaming of this drop all the previous night, knowing that the other two had made it was small consolation, particularly when there was no choice, no real way to portage. Down the first shoot, over the small drop, spin in the slack water and then over the fall, hard left and moving left to avoid the water slamming into the cliff face opposite. I seemed to be in the air for ages, falling from the light into the dark cave below. And then it was over. Safe once more, my heart still hammering, the adrenaline still surging, as I looked back at the fall. It was twice as high as Dave had said when he had explained the line in our tiny eddy high above – but then again honesty is not always a virtue, what was the point in scaring me beforehand?

We continued on downstream, feeling relaxed and confident but still very alert. Providing we hadn't missed anything on the scout, the biggest drops were now behind us and there were just a couple more bouldery rapids, some more 20 foot shoots and that last river-wide ledge. And sure enough, everything went sweetly. Some four hours after entering the gorge, we emerged, triumphant. Exhausted physically and mentally, we left our boats on the sandy beach at the take-out, and made our way up to the sun loungers on the veranda of the only restaurant for miles around. It was New Year's Eve, and four very happy kayakers swilled cool beer around their glasses and dreamt of the next three weeks and the rivers that were still to come. Boating in Chile was going to be fun.

ABOVE, IN THE LAND OF
THE LILLIPUTIANS
ON THE RIO PALGUIN.
RIGHT, ON THE 'SIETE TAZAS'
(SEVEN TEACUPS), RIO CLARO.

Andy was in the habit of noting details of rivers he had paddled or hoped to paddle in a variety of notebooks. Under the Rio Claro he observes: "Fernando, the Park Ranger with a moustache, has a key to the track (river right). Bring him Scotch Whisky!"

Sometimes the notebooks contain details of who owes whom money and occasionally entries were made in somebody else's hand. There is a comment on the Rio Peusco: "... supposed to be a full on grade 5. Put on at the bridge for a 5km run. The police chased us away." This event seems to have inspired observations on the Chilean police and AJ himself, written by fast jet pilot Dave Landie.

Insight into Chilean culture No. 1

With the demise of the Pinochet era picking on the intellectual classes has obviously become unfashionable in Chile.

Being working class themselves, the police are therefore limited to persecuting the lowest social order... kayakers.

To this end, and having taken great care to wait until we had fully unloaded the pickup and were all but ready to throw ourselves headlong into the Peusco, two of Chile's finest sauntered down the road from their border checkpoint looking like a bizarre cross between Mussolini and Sgt Bilko. I say sauntered yet they probably weren't even that fast. Not that that mattered because they were still easily within the time frame Andy required for his habitual pre-river running ritual of whingeing about his back, stretching and pulling it back into alignment with all accompanying creeks and groans, whingeing about his upset stomach, clearing the aforementioned so violently as to put his back out, whingeing about his back, stretching and pulling it... ad nauseum.

You can forgive these guys for not crediting us with the intellectual ability that fifteen years ago would have assured our position at the head of the torture queue at the local football stadium since the ensuing conversation went something like this:

First, from our point of view.

Carabineros: Wild and graphic gesticulations signifying certain death in the canyon below by means of either a smashed face, two broken arms, a severed torso and two broken legs.

A run-in with Zoro.

We were none too sure which but since the end result was the same we decided not to prolong the guys' clearly uncomfortable (but extremely funny) contortionist act. All, that is, except Andy who, having somehow construed this gruesome portrayal as 'the nod', gave our two carabineros a winning smile, two big thumbs up and started to drag his boat to the waters' edge.

From the Carabineros' point of view we can only assume that the exchange went something like this:

Son of Pinochet: No

Gormless, lanky, apparently stupid kayaker: Something unintelligible in a foreign tongue.

Son of Pinochet: No, absolutely not. You will die terribly and I will have to remove your body parts from the "Gorge of a thousand gruesome deaths". So no!

Andy: See above

Son of Pinochet: I am a policeman. In Chile when a policeman says "no" it means no!

Andy: So it's ok then?

Whether smart enough to warrant being shot or stupid enough to be allowed to die in the gorge, even Andy understood our now frustrated policeman's brutal mime of our imminent arrest and what might subsequently happen in custody.

We learned two things from this cultural exchange.

Chilean policemen would probably be very good at charades.

If Chilean policemen spent more time fighting crime and less time amusing tourists we probably would not have had our car broken into.

A number of other themes from Jackson's life are also reprised in the notebook; his awareness of wee tracks up river banks, as sharp as a burglar's eye for an open window; his occasionally strained relations with the 'Polis' and other access incidents.

ABOVE, LAUNCH AT KORCHON.

RIGHT, PADDLING ON THE MARSYANGDI.

FLYING FISH

Round about 1998 a mountain guide called Bruce Poll came to live with Andy. Eventually he moved out, built himself a house and was reinvented as Bruce the Builder. Before he swapped the lure of the hills for vertical walls of a more prosaic sort Bruce passed on his other passion to the inmates of Whinknowe. He is a paraglider. There is a story of Bruce landing his £2,000 wing on a sheep infested hillside, panicking a ewe which bolted into the billowing material, thrashing around there until she had completely destroyed it. This is a sport best pursued on sunny, sheepless days with light winds and is clearly ideal for Fort William. To the incurable optimist it could seem a good option for days when the Lochaber weather wasn't right for boating or skiing. The bug bit not only Andy, and therefore Bridget but also Big Al Collis and Stew Rogers, the avalanche man. Andy had developed a mysteriously sore right wrist. He could not remember hurting it but it simply did not get better. Medical science could offer no explanation and he was forced to consider becoming a left handed paddler but in the meantime paragliding seemed to offer an exciting way to spend the summer. Before long they were dropping in among the criss-crossed power lines in our field.

Andy's approach to flying seemed very similar to his kayaking. Meticulous planning, careful attention to detail, care of equipment and observation of conditions are obviously good habits to cultivate in a sport which offers the possibility of falling thousands of feet to earth. They quickly passed their club pilots' licence and soon a flood of stories demonstrated the possibilities of the sport. On one of his early flights Big Al Collis took off from the Aonach Mòr ski area and flew to Bridge of Orchy, 23 miles as the glider flies but about 45 miles by road. Rejecting the possibility of a longer flight into Perthshire he opted to land by the road and began to hitch. The first car that arrived gave him a lift right to the door. There were also reports of thermals carrying them up Ben Nevis above the footpath, offering encouragement to the sweating masses toiling up hill over the scree, and eventually circling 2,000 feet above the summit. It was also possible take off near the Glen Coe ski area and fly down the glen parallel to the top of the spectacular Aonach Eagach, again having conversations with climbers on the ridge.

At the end of the first summer Andy and Bid went to Mexico to hone their skills. In January of 2000 they were back in Nepal, a familiar happy hunting ground of numerous kayaking trips. Bridget decided not to abort a take off that didn't seem right, crashed and suffered a nasty double fracture of a lower leg. X-rays showed a crush fracture of her spinal vertebrae but this wasn't noticed until she got back to Scotland. Her back gives her pain to this day. Andy's log for the day is notably brief. It simply states "Bid's crash". After the crash Andy carried on flying while Bid sat around in plaster and waited. There are those that suggest that Andy was inclined to take Bridget for granted and wasn't always very considerate of her. Bridget herself would reject this, to a degree. Andy didn't know that her back was injured. If he had broken his leg he would not have expected everybody else to stop playing. When Bid broke a finger during an 'extreme race' on the Nevis he immediately scratched from the race, took her to hospital and was the model concerned partner. On the other hand, when Bridget was working in far off Dundee she would sometimes make it back to Banavie for the weekend to find Andy about to depart with a group of the lads for a weekend of hard paddling, which she was welcome to join, if she wanted. After a week of hard work and a three hour drive she often wanted something less demanding. The top performers in outdoor sports rarely make stereotype good partners. Some of them, like Dougal Haston, are self confessed selfish bastards. One of Audrey Whillans friends said: "I wouldn't go so far as to say that Audrey never had a kid. She just never gave birth to one", a penetrating verdict on life with the Don, probably Salford's greatest ever climber. Nobody gets to the top without being driven to perform and to excel and inevitably there are sacrifices. There can also be compensations and Bridget is familiar with both sides of the coin. Towards the end of his life, as his energy was sapped he consistently encouraged her to paddle or ski with whoever was available and frequently I was the lucky man. When ill he never seemed down or sought to share his misery with others. Denise Marriot, a freelance outdoor instructor and paddling friend of Andy and Bid, commented on his "obsessive water level checking and constant nagging... there was not a relaxing day to be had in the house when it rained, even if he couldn't go himself!" Good days are a finite resource and they should not be wasted.

After a summer trip to Norway with Callum Anderson, Dec 2001 saw Andy back in Nepal. Dave Kwant told the story in an article on *Canoe & Kayak UK*.

High Times and Flying Fish

Nothing can prepare you for the experience of walking out of the airport at Kathmandu. Imagine being a superstar at some high-profile event, except the crowd barriers are not there to keep the Paparazzi at bay. Instead they hold back the throngs of taxi drivers all shouting and trying desperately to get hold of something belonging to you that they can put in their taxi to guarantee a fare. As Andy, Bridget and I spilled into the sunshine, the pandemonium was broken by a large, slightly hunched figure that waded through the crowds and with a few words of Nepali, momentarily silenced the hoards. This was Big Al, a paddling buddy and tandem paraglider pilot from the UK, now resident in Canada. In the days to come he was to be the man in charge of getting my camera and me off terra firma and high into the Himalayan sky. For this was to be a boating holiday with a difference.

It was all part of a cunning plan hatched at a party in Fort William in the Scottish Highlands two years earlier. Andy and Bridget, whose home we had invaded, had dreams of combining two of their favourite pastimes into one epic trip. Fresh from their most recent paragliding holiday in Nepal, the plan involved a long paraglide flight across the Himalayas, followed by a three-day kayak trip back to civilization. This sounded wicked, so despite never having been near a paraglider in my life, I signed up immediately as trip cameraman. That night I went to sleep dreaming of paddling Himalayan whitewater and drifting like a leaf in a gentle breeze, with a backdrop of stunning snow-covered mountains.

However, the reality of paragliding was to prove somewhat different. Standing at a take-off site high above the town of Pokhara, my hands started to tremble. With Al in charge our launch went surprisingly well. On his command, I leant forward into the harness and threw my weight into running down the hill. The glider gently lifted us up and off, the ground fell away, and we were flying. What a feeling! Then something happened that I really didn't expect. We hit a thermal; the glider lurched backwards then steadied before we banked right as Al piloted us to stay within the pocket of rising air. Despite all the talk, nothing had prepared me for the force of the hot air exploding upwards as we had hit the thermal. Unfortunately, my stomach had expected nothing of the sort either and despite my best efforts to keep my breakfast where it belonged, this bizarre environment was too much for my body to handle and the offending breakfast was jettisoned with some force. Coming into land, I again felt my stomach revolt, but managed to keep my mouth closed and swallowed hard. My dreams of gentle floating had been smashed; I had just had my first lesson in paragliding and thermals.

The next few weeks passed in fine style. We were joined by Alex, another keen paddler and cameraman,

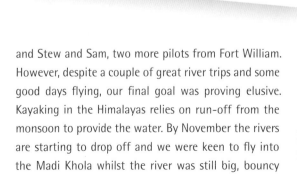

and Stew and Sam, two more pilots from Fort William. However, despite a couple of great river trips and some good days flying, our final goal was proving elusive. Kayaking in the Himalayas relies on run-off from the monsoon to provide the water. By November the rivers are starting to drop off and we were keen to fly into the Madi Khola whilst the river was still big, bouncy and fun. However, it's not until a few months after the monsoon that you get classic paragliding conditions, with thermals strong enough to allow you to gain height and attempt long cross country flights.

As the days passed our carefree attitude began to change. Day by day the flying was improving, but not only that, our flights home were looming and with three days needed for the river trip, we calculated that we had just two days left to attempt to paraglide to the put-in. After that we would just have to take the more conventional approach and walk. A new focus was needed if we were to complete our mission. The next morning we waved goodbye to Alex, who along with our newly employed porters was to shepherd our boats to the put-in.

We packed everything from our hotel room into storage and set off to make a serious attempt at the long flight. Despite several breakdowns, our two battered 30-year-old Toyota Corollas finally disgorged us at the take-off zone. We quickly unpacked and Bridget was the first to launch, almost immediately connecting with a good thermal and disappearing off on the first leg of the flight. Finally, after all the waiting, today was going to be the day.

But our hopes were short-lived, and it was not to be. Bridget's was the last good thermal of the day. And less than an hour later, as the clouds built up and the thermals disappeared, we were all back on the ground in the landing area below take-off. Back at the hotel we were met with gales of good-natured laughter from the Nepali hotel owners as we got all our kit back out

of storage. There was nothing for it but to head over to Guru's Restaurant for commiseration and a drink or two.

Day two dawned bright and sunny and our spirits rose as we once again bounced along to the take-off. We launched one at a time, and flew backwards and forwards along the ridge, hoping to connect with a good thermal and gain height. After an hour of 'scratching' in close to the trees, Andy and Stew got good climbs and made the first big leap of the flight. Bridget, Al and myself were still cruising the take-off ridge, alternately kicking trees and gaining height above the ridge. By now, Andy and Stew could only just be seen as small dots of fabric cruising along the huge green jungle wall behind us.

And then we hooked a good climb. We circled in the thermal, gaining altitude, getting excited; the first leg was in the bag. But then disaster struck! The thermal seemed to peter out, we widened our circle desperately looking for the lifting air, but within minutes we were back down at take-off height, hugging the cliff, the wing tip only inches from the trees as Al fought to keep us aloft.

By now the day was starting to cloud over. Andy and Stew had long disappeared out of sight and out of radio contact over the back of the next ridge. We would have no way of contacting them again and finding out whether they had crashed or made it to the put-in, until we got there ourselves that is. As conditions deteriorated, we made a desperate bid to fly to the big face behind us where the air should be lifting better. But we weren't high enough, and soon found ourselves dropping rapidly towards the valley floor as we hit sinking air.

And then it was all over. We hit the ground with a thump, too tired to even stand, and were immediately surrounded by curious children delighted that we had dropped into their back garden. We packed up, and made our way to the waiting taxi, where we found Bridget with a similar story to tell. Completely exhausted from the flight, both physically and mentally, and disappointed not to have achieved our goal, we resigned ourselves to the walk-in. To make matters worse, we could only imagine the glee with which we would once more be greeted back at the hotel.

Meanwhile Andy had found some good lift on the wall as expected and had popped over the ridge at its lowest point, through a small gap in the cloud. Finding himself in a steep sided valley densely covered in trees, and with no possible landing sites, he was relieved to see Stew ahead of him, just about to drop over the next ridge into the Madi Khola valley. By the narrowest of margins, Andy managed to glide over the steep sided jungle of the following ridge and he too arrived in the Madi Khola valley. Below him, in a flat paddy field, Alex was waiting with the kayaks. The mission was still on.

Next morning there was no option for Al, Bridget and myself, but to admit defeat and walk to the put-in. So with sinking hearts, we jumped once again into our knackered taxi and set off towards the river. The drive proved almost as dangerous as the flying with water coming in over the sills as the taxi crossed braided river beds and teetered up narrow dirt tracks with alarming drop-offs. But eventually, the road disintegrated too much and it was time to walk.

It was a relief to finally meet up with the others at the put-in of the river, to have the whole team back together and catch up with each other's adventures. Stew still had the walk-out to come and, having seen something of the river, was disappointed to have left his kayak back in Scotland. But there was little time to waste; we had a deadline to meet.

We packed our boats and waved goodbye to the crowds of local people who had come to see us off and share the festival atmosphere. From the put-in, the rapids down to Souda were steep and technical. Progress was slow as we scouted and filmed. This gave our Nepali spectators plenty of opportunity to keep pace with us, and some of the crowd followed for miles, cheering from the high terraces. Absorbed in the river, we barely noticed the passing of time. All too soon the light began to fade. With the onset of dusk we put away the cameras and picked up the pace, boat scouting our way down the steep grade 4 boulder fields.

The lack of light also reminded us that it was time to find a place to sleep. One of the beauties of kayaking in Nepal is the sandy beach-like camping spots left as the rivers drop. Finding a nice beach that also catches the early morning sunshine can however be quite an art form, especially if you don't want your every move, waking and sleeping, watched by a large and curious crowd of locals.

Soon we were comfortably settled, with little to do but stir the dinner and watch the stars – savouring the thought of the river ahead and at peace with ourselves. Morning arrived and with it a crowd of Nepali children.

With no bridge for miles they could only shout and waves to us from the opposite bank. This proved sufficiently entertaining for both parties and they watched us for the two hours it took for us to get on the river. Finally their patience was rewarded as we went over to say hello before heading off downstream. They watched with rapt attention until we disappeared out of sight and into more of the same technical kayaking that we had enjoyed the day before. By now we had a good rhythm going and the group was working well together as a team. The rapids were a mixture of grades 3 and 4, and we made fast progress.

By the end of the third morning, the last of the rapids started to flatten out and we could feel the river easing itself into a new frame of mind. The continuous charge downhill had lessened to become a very gentle amble along the flood plains at the bottom of the valley. This marked the start of the dreaded flat section. It was one o'clock in the afternoon. With 26km of flat water now lying between the road and us, there was nothing for it. We had to grit our teeth and paddle hard for a full four hours to get to the take-out in time for the last bus of the day. We needed to be back in Pokhara that night if Alex, who flew out first, was to make his international flight, and the thought of a good meal and cold beers at Guru's was like a mirage in front of our eyes as we slogged down the endless flat section.

Arriving at the final beach at last, we were pleased to see a crowd of Nepalis digging up the sand and taking it away in a very old tractor. After some brief negotiations we threw the kayaks on the back of the trailer and

started inching our way up the steep bank. This brought us out in the village of Damauli. Keen to show off the 'catch of the day', our friends paraded us through the village at a snail's pace, hollering to all their mates to come and see this bizarre collection of humans they had found by the river.

Only now did we realise that we had actually done it. The strange idea that had caused a large amount of ridicule and laughter at the party in Fort William two years previously had happened. One thing was true; it had all been way more bizarre and fun than we could ever have imagined.

ANDY ABOVE THE CLOUDS, EVENING AT KORCHON.

To many observers this style of expedition reeks of western self-indulgence. One view is of wealthy young Europeans arriving in poverty stricken third world countries, having burned unthinkable amounts of aviation fuel to get there. They are equipped with a bewildering array of the latest expensive shiny toys, which they pay pathetically grateful and desperately undernourished locals a miserly pittance to carry up to the starting point of their great adventure. When not amusing themselves they patronize children who come to gaze on the peculiar bodies, wealth and madness of the strangers. Their exertions give them an insatiable appetite and they demand and pay for so much food that poorer natives find themselves cut out of the food chain. When they go they take only memories and leave only footprints, piles of packaging, rubbish, oxygen cylinders, bodies and a variety of interesting infectious diseases. Meanwhile growing budget air transport is an ever more important cause of carbon emissions and climate change.

There is, inevitably, a degree of truth in this and everybody who has ever lived or worked in a third world country will be aware of embarrassing disparities of wealth. Andy did a huge amount of travelling and if he had felt inclined to defend his lifestyle he might have pointed out that tourism, for all its obvious defects, gives people in countries like Nepal access to western products, like medicine that they would not otherwise get near. Porters and others working for westerners always get paid more than they would working for locals. There never seems to be a shortage of people willing to do these jobs and there are very good reasons for this. Outdoor sports tourism has created new lives and lifestyles. Nepal and Uganda have home grown whitewater stars, Morocco has Berber ski guides, Giriama windsurfing dudes make a living on the Kenya coast by hiring gear and giving lessons. A love of outdoor adrenalin is not purely a western phenomenon. Andy had a fairly frugal lifestyle. Neither he nor Bridget were dedicated followers of fashion and his annual clothes budget would not have seemed extravagant in Kampala or Kathmandu. He didn't spend a lot on gear; kind people generally gave it to him. He shared his home with many others thus saving on heating and energy. He said he didn't drink very much and he certainly didn't smoke. Kerosene was his one vice and, to be fair, most of his flying took place before the current awareness of the impact of aviation on climate. If the tourist industry dries up world wide there will be many who suffer in the less prosperous parts of the planet.

Dave Kwant's abiding memory of the trip is of Andy's suspect diet. His preference was for cheap Nepali versions of western food, like Lasagne. Kwant is deeply suspicious of the ingredients, especially the cheese, which he thinks was probably the origins of Andy's brucellosis. On his first trip to Nepal this diet did not agree well with Dave. On subsequent visits he sustained himself on dalbat, a nourishing mixture of locally grown lentils and rice, and found himself feeling much better. In Kwant's opinion Andy's daily consumption of up to six tablets of Voltarin, high strength Ibuprofen to keep him playing could only have had a seriously deleterious effect on his digestion and general health. Bridget insists that he was only taking medication prescribed for him and that the lasagne would have been well cooked in the oven and should have been hot enough to be germ free. One way or another, however, Andy did get brucellosis and it cost him, and Scottish sport, dear.

ANDY JACKSON
1971 – 2004.

THE LEGACY

Andy's death has never been explained by medical science. A number of the factors are known but no complete explanation exists. It all seemed to begin in 1997 with a sore wrist. He couldn't explain how it came to be sore and neither his GP nor his physio could understand what was wrong. It went in time to be replaced by pain in the pelvis and lower back caused by a misunderstanding with a tree while skiing. This eventually cleared up but he began to suffer from a lack of energy which was alarmingly like ME.

On his 2001 paragliding and kayaking trip to Nepal he appears to have contracted brucellosis. This may have happened on a previous trip to Nepal in 1999 or even Turkey in 1997. However he only became obviously ill with flu like symptoms in February 2002, about 6 weeks after returning from his last trip to Nepal. Tested for every other complaint, the problem was not diagnosed until 2002. Brucellosis, sometimes called contagious abortion, is an illness that needs to be diagnosed and treated quickly.

Mortality from brucellosis alone is only about 2% but it is not easy to eliminate it from the system. He suffered from painful hips that are a common symptom of the complaint. After long courses of very aggressive antibiotics Andy was clear of it but he did not recover his previous energy levels. Nevertheless he continued to paddle and in a knackered, sick state could still get down rivers that would scare many witless. In the last year of his life he paddled the entire upper Nevis and took himself to the brink of exhaustion running all that is paddlable of the Fassfern. At other times his lack of energy was more apparent. He got on the Garry, intending to have a quiet day, and discovered that even this was beyond him. Drifting past the playhole of which he was once the undisputed master, he floated down to Whitebridge and got out immediately with a look of relief. On the first occasion he had taken me to that river in 1990 we paddled the whole thing, right down to the old bridge three or four times, running the shuttle with a bike. It was an alarming change.

Not long after his death, in response to requests from grieving friends, Bridget wrote about the latter stages of his illness.

As the months went by Andy seemed to gradually get a little better. I went on a ski holiday without him in March 2003, but by October that year he felt well enough to go to the Grand Canyon (which was a good mellow trip - lots of riding on rafts). The following March, we went skiing with friends in France. Andy managed between two and five hours skiing a day - not quite the eight or more hour days we would normally do, but pretty good. In June we went to a friends wedding in Italy and went paragliding. I guess that was probably Andy at his fittest.

By the autumn Andy felt his recovery had levelled off. In November he spent a few days with a friend in France (Stew Rogers) paragliding and managed to fly most days, even if briefly.

I had holiday left to take, so we planned a week's flying in Spain in December and then a ski trip over Christmas and New Year. We thought a week away from the computer and chilling out would do him good. Any flying would be a bonus. Andy felt very tired and did not go out paddling or flying the weekend before we went away.

We arrived in Spain on Saturday evening (27th November) in time to go out for some food. Next morning Andy was tired but not unusually so for a bad day. Sunday we flew for about thirty minutes in the late afternoon. The conditions weren't great, and it required a lot of concentration to use the patches of lift to stay flying. After landing Andy said he was exhausted. We packed up and waited to be collected. That night Andy was tired, so we ate in and got an early night.

Andy woke up next day (Monday) feeling very ill. Alternately feverish and cold with a splitting headache. We thought maybe the travelling had been too much, maybe he was tired, he had had a beer Saturday night, which maybe didn't agree with the medication. But basically we thought he was just more ill than usual and that a day lying on the couch would sort him out.

Tuesday Andy was the same (I went flying for an hour). I went and bought some paracetamol and Andy sent a text to a doctor friend to ask about taking this with his medication. Amy sent a text back saying it sounded like Andy had flu and paracetamol was fine with his other drugs.

Andy was the same again Wednesday. He said he felt no worse, but no better. I called the person who was looking after us, and he organised a doctor's appointment. His wife came along to translate. The doctor took Andy's blood pressure, temperature, listened to his chest and took a urine sample. He said he had flu and prescribed some medication to help his digestion and some tablets, which were basically vitamin C and paracetamol. He was eating very little, but was managing a little food and was drinking constantly.

By Thursday morning Andy said he'd had an awful night, but that he still just felt as bad as he had all week. On Friday we decided to fly home but could not get direct flights. Instead we had to go through East Midlands Airport. Andy looked really tired and ill by this time with his eyes red and bloodshot.

As we expected the journey was tiring, particularly with a five hour stop over at East Midlands Airport. Andy was drinking lots, and managed a few mouthfuls of food. I phoned Andy's parents in Glasgow and said we were coming home early (we were supposed to fly on Monday), and they said that they would collect us. Andy was keen to get to Fort William, so I said that we might not stay the night. Andy phoned his GP in Fort William and made an appointment for Monday.

We got to Glasgow around 10 pm. Andy was knackered, so we went back to his parents and crashed for the night.

Next morning Andy said that he had not slept and had spent half the night sitting in the living room. We thought that a doctor would just confirm that Andy had flu and that as a virus this was untreatable, but decided that maybe we should see a doctor before heading on up the road. I rang the local out of hours' number and got NHS twenty-four. They asked some questions then rang back. Eventually they gave us a choice of an appointment or a home visit at some point during the day. Andy said that he would go in, so at 10 am we arrived for his appointment at the Royal Alexandria. We arrived at the wrong building and Andy was so weak he asked for a wheelchair and I pushed him over to see the GP. The GP examined him and said she would like the hospital doctors to look at him. So off we went back to triage and then to an examination room. A junior house officer took his blood pressure and listened to his chest. His blood pressure was around 75/53, and his blood oxygen 80ish. They said that Andy was very dehydrated accounting for his low blood pressure and that his breathing was fast and shallow. Because of this and his low blood oxygen, they did a chest x-ray which showed pneumonia – I'm sure they said that the x-ray showed a small infection in one lung.

Andy was put on a drip and oxygen mask. He was worried, particularly by the oxygen, but I was confident that everything that needed to be happening was. Andy's blood pressure went up a little and so did his oxygen levels and they reduced the O2 pressure a little. A more senior doctor also came to see Andy.

At around 3 pm, Andy was admitted to the ward. His parents came in and we stayed to the end of visiting around 4 pm. We were told that a ward round would start soon, and Andy would see a consultant. I think it was after the ward round that Andy was given intravenous antibiotics.

At 7 pm I came back for visiting hours, and stayed until they eventually threw me out around 9 pm. I had taken more books with me for Andy to read. We sat together quietly but said all the important things. Andy had had around 7 x 500ml bags of fluid by this time, both glucose and saline.

I got back to Andy's parents to hear that they had called the hospital and been told that Andy was being moved to the high dependency unit overnight as that way someone would be keeping a close eye on him. They said that Andy had not responded as they had hoped, but seemed confident that he would.

We all went to bed. At 12.30 we got a call to say that Andy had been moved to intensive care, where he would receive one to one nursing. His nurse Gerry explained that they had sedated him and put him on a ventilator, to make sure that his body got sufficient oxygen and allow it to concentrate on fighting the infection. Gerry said that if we wished to see what was happening we could go in, but that we did not need to at this stage.

Andy's mum Kate and I went to the hospital. Gerry said that there was a chance that Andy would not make it but gave him a 99.9% chance of full recovery, even if he needed to spend some time in intensive care.

Andy's blood tests showed that his kidneys and liver were failing and so dialysis was started. This affected his blood pressure. Various drugs were used to counteract this and to help him in other ways.

Gerry said that they had to keep escalating the levels of drugs used, but still Andy did not stabilise. At around 5 am Gerry suggested that Kate call Andy's brothers and sisters. Three came in, and the other two started the journey.

The staff then put Andy on a very powerful type of ventilator called an oscillator. Again this did not improve Andy's levels of blood oxygen and at this point we were told that his chances were very slim. We all said our goodbyes and Kate phoned Andy's sisters in England to let them know that they were going to be too late.

Andy died some time around 6.30 am.

During the night Gerry had explained that they had not at first realised how sick Andy was. Young people compensate when they are ill, so if part of the body is not working right other parts compensate allowing them to keep going and not show how ill they really are. Gerry said that Andy should not have been able to string two words together when he came in and should barely have been conscious. Instead of which he was joking and gave Gerry a thumbs up and a wink.

I'm glad that we had that last week together – talking, reading, holding hands – during which we felt very close. I'm pleased that Andy didn't become frustrated with a body that did not allow him to do the things that he so passionately wanted to. And I'm grateful that I did not watch him drown, or break apart on a hillside and that, once in hospital, the responsibly for doing the right thing was not mine alone. He died with his parents and family, not in a Spanish hospital, where we would not have understood what was happening.

His extensive circle of friends was stunned by his death, even if they weren't entirely surprised. Three years after the event Bridget has, with difficulty, learned to live with her loss. What then is the legacy of this remarkable man?

He has left behind an astonishing number of tall tales that people tell about him. Returning from the Topo Rally in Augsburg he had a couple of spare Topos to take back on the plane. Arriving at the last minute for check in with Lufthansa he told Dave Kwant to stay out of sight with the boats until called. Dave was doubtful but complied. Minutes later he heard Andy calling, "Dave, hurry up with those bags!" The check in girl was aghast as Andy insisted that these were the bags he had told her about and while she was distracted he leaned across the desk and helped himself to the tickets she had printed for the bags. With the plane due to fly and checked in luggage still to board she was flustered into agreement and two Topos were loaded as hold baggage.

Clad in smelly fleeces, Jackson and Kwant found themselves seated with passengers in sharp suits being offered free champagne and steak by the trolley dollies. The late check in had resulted in their being upgraded to first class as all economy seats had been allocated. If he is to be remembered, though, it will be for something more than scams, no matter how hilarious or outrageous.

With his legacy of exploratory kayaking we are on fairly safe ground. Nobody has ever done so many new rivers in Scotland and it's unlikely that anybody else will do more in future. A feeling persists, though, that he has left others more aware of the possibilities that imagination, new gear and new techniques may offer to take the sport into new territory. The guidebooks and the videos are a valuable if partial record of this legacy. But important as these things are, they are not the whole story.

Many of those who wrote to Bridget after Andy's death described him as inspirational. Some of this came from the World Tour, which opened eyes and horizons to kayakers across the UK and beyond. It began the whitewater equivalent of the hippy trail.

Gary Tompsett, extreme endurance athlete and event organizer sees the inspirational aspect on an even higher plane. "The way that he would always give something to you, in a spiritual sense. Energy, renewed hope, vision, purpose, support. Even in the shortest meetings. Rare in a world where most people seem to take some of those things away." Gary would probably agree that Andy would be better remembered for his humour than his personal hygiene. Tompsett was convulsed: "When he recounted his tales of amoebic dysentery whilst travelling in buses in Nepal. Graphic but hilarious. I imagine it was an often repeated (and skilfully told) story." There must be a warning there for us all.

Denise Marriot believes that: "Andy accepted everyone, even climbers sometimes! He paddled without ego and seemed endlessly motivated to coach others around him either on the river or on the slopes; it never really seemed to be about him. To me he represented inspiration, safety, kindness, energy, fun, caring, modest, a big long person with big long arms that always welcomed people in, unique."

Andy travelled a great deal and those who accompanied him often comment on how people seemed to know him wherever he went. More than that people liked him and often wanted to be like him and in their emulating his values and attitudes he has probably influenced the whole ethos of Scottish Kayaking. It had strong instincts to inclusiveness long before Andy came on the scene; he fed on these and then helped them to grow and develop to be central to the ethos of the sport. One of the tributes written at the time of his funeral simply said:

"He was a role model to so many of us... An infectious enthusiasm would lead you across wind swept moorland carrying 20kg of plastic and enjoying the adventure of it all. When things went pear shaped a smiling and encouraging face would greet you, never making you feel stupid or embarrassed about that swim. When you paddled with him you knew you had him watching over your blind side. Like many people I will try to keep alive a little of Andy in what I do and in what I try to pass on to others."

Since he became ill and since his death paddling has moved on in Scotland and beyond. Kayakers are running drops that Andy looked at and walked away from. Davie Biggin's descents of the Falls of Clyde and the Hermitage both come in this category. Yet Andy's exploratory paddling has provided the base from which much of current developments stem and his example the inspiration. As teenagers Tom Brown and David Broadley used to come to Banavie at weekends, stay in Andy's caravan and paddle with Big Al Collis or Andy himself. Tom, who is credited with the only known descent of Madness on the Affric, a fall which Jackson walked, remembers with enthusiasm the encouragement, help and lift he got from these contacts. Part of Andy's legacy is to be seen in the way that other paddlers, influenced by him, have taken the sport on to new levels.

Andy himself would be embarrassed by this. He rarely talked about the things he had done. He enjoyed recognition and having a reputation but that wasn't really what drove him. Olaf Obsommer believes: "The best paddler in the world is the paddler who has the most fun." Andy certainly got a lot of fun out of his boating and from the friendship that went with it. Of all the things he was good at he was probably best at friendship. For a man who was always laughing and joking he was amazingly quick to realize when others needed support and was generous in giving it. If his legacy is to remind us that boating is about friendship and fun rather than self aggrandisement he would probably be happy to settle for that and few occasions do more to bring fun and friendship to the fore than the whitewater weekend that was started in his memory and which gives paddlers guaranteed weekend access to the Garry and the Morriston each September. It is the sort of event where he would have been completely in his element, enjoying the company of others and their pleasure in two of Scotland's most beautiful whitewater rivers.

On hearing of his death in New Zealand Dave Kwant and Steve Rogers summed up what many felt:

"Now that he is gone, I can't quite put a finger on what is missing ... I think I miss his long arms most of all. They were always there if you needed a hug and always there if you needed a helping hand.

They were there at every party swaying above everybody like a big tree, and they were stretched out when you needed a beer. When we were kayaking together I remember joking about how long his arms looked, how he always seemed to reach the bank wherever he was. But most of all I remember how those long arms were always waiting in the last eddy with a huge grin behind them... He was my hero."

In Memory Of
Andy Jackson
1971 – 2004

A World renowned
White Water Kayaker
who learned to paddle here
at Castle Semple Loch.

THE COMMEMORATIVE
STONE AT THE
LOCHSIDE WHERE ANDY
LEARNT TO CANOE.

ANDY SURFS THE
FOREVER WAVE,
FALLS OF LORA.